blankets bears and **bootees**

Quadrille
PUBLISHING

blankets bears and bootees

20 irresistible hand knits for your baby

Debbie Bliss

photography by Ulla Nyeman

knitting basics 8

patterns 36

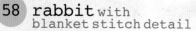

a box of bootees

knitting basics

types of yarns

When choosing a yarn for children's hand knits it is important that you work with a fibre that is soft but also practical. Children are often more used to the lightweight freedom of fleeces, and they can be resistant to hand knits that they may consider scratchy and uncomfortable.

The yarns I have chosen for the designs in this book are either an extra fine merino or cashmere mixes. Although they create fabrics that are gentle against the skin, the other essential feature is that they are machine washable.

When knitting a garment always make the effort to buy the yarn stated in the pattern. All these designs have been created with a specific yarn in mind. A different yarn may not produce the same quality of fabric or have the same wash and wear properties. From an aesthetic point of view, the clarity of a subtle stitch pattern may be lost if a garment is knitted in an inferior yarn.

However, there may be occasions when a knitter needs to substitute a yarn – if there is an allergy to wool, for example – and so the following is a guideline to making the most informed choices.

Always buy a yarn that is the same weight as that given in the pattern: replace a double knitting with a double knitting, for example, and check that the tension of both yarns is the same.

Where you are substituting a different fibre, be aware of the design. A cable pattern knitted in cotton when worked in wool will pull in because of the greater elasticity of the yarn and so the fabric will become narrower; this will alter the proportions of the garment.

Check the metreage of the yarn. Yarns that weigh the same may have different lengths in the ball or hank, so you may need to buy more or less yarn.

Here are descriptions of my yarns and a guide to their weights and types:

Debbie Bliss baby cashmerino:
A lightweight yarn between a 4ply and a double knitting.
55% merino wool, 33% microfibre, 12% cashmere.
Approximately 125m/50g ball.
Debbie Bliss cashmerino aran:
55% merino wool, 33% microfibre, 12% cashmere.
Approximately 90m/50g ball.
Debbie Bliss cashmerino double knitting:
55% merino wool, 33% microfibre, 12% cashmere.
Approximately 110m/50g ball.
Debbie Bliss rialto double knitting:
100% merino wool extra fine superwash.
Approximately 105m/50g ball.

Debbie Bliss rialto aran:
100% merino wool extra fine superwash.
Approximately 80m/50g ball.

buying yarn

The ball band on the yarn will carry all the essential information you need as to tension, needle size, weight and yardage. Importantly, it will also have a dye lot number. Yarns are dyed in batches or lots, which can vary considerably. As your retailer may not have the same dye lot later on, buy all your yarn for a project at the same time. If you know that sometimes you use more yarn than that quoted in a pattern, buy extra. If it is not possible to buy all the yarn you need with the same dye lot number, use the different ones where the shade change will not show as much, on a neck or border, as a change of dye lot across a main piece will most likely show.

It is also a good idea at the time of buying the yarn that you check the pattern and make sure that you already have the needles you will require. If not, buy them now, as it will save a lot of frustration when you get home.

garment care

Taking care of your hand knits is important because you want them to look good for as long as possible. Correct washing is particularly important for children's garments as they need to be washed often.

Check the ball band on the yarn for washing instructions to see whether the yarn is hand or machine washable, and if it is the latter, at what temperature it should be washed.

Most hand knits should be dried flat on an absorbent cloth, such as a towel, to soak up any moisture. Laying them flat in this way gives you an opportunity to pat the garment back into shape if it has become pulled around in the washing machine. Even if you are in a hurry, do not be tempted to dry your knits near a direct heat source, such as a radiator.

As children's garments are small, you may prefer to hand wash them. Use a washing agent that is specifically designed for knitwear as this will be kinder to the fabric. Use warm rather than hot water and handle the garment gently without rubbing or wringing. Let the water out of the basin and then gently squeeze out the excess water. Do not lift out a water-logged knit as the weight of the water will pull it out of shape. You may need to remove more moisture by rolling in a towel. Dry flat as before.

techniques

cast on

Your first step when beginning to knit is to work a foundation row called a cast-on. Without this row you cannot begin to knit.

There are several methods of casting on, each can be suited to a particular purpose or is chosen because the knitter feels comfortable with that particular technique. The two examples that follow are the ones I have found to be the most popular, the thumb and the cable methods.

In order to work a cast-on edge, you must first make a slip-knot.

slip-knot

1 Wind the yarn around the fingers on your left hand to make a circle of yarn as shown above. With the knitting needle, pull a loop of the yarn attached to the ball through the yarn circle on your fingers.

2 Pull both ends of the yarn to tighten the slip-knot on the knitting needle. You are now ready to begin, using either of the following cast-on techniques.

cast on

thumb cast-on

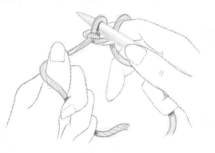

1 Make a slip-knot as shown on page 15, leaving a long tail. With the slip-knot on the needle in your right hand and the yarn that comes from the ball over your index finger, wrap the tail end of the yarn over your left thumb from front to back, holding the yarn in your palm with your fingers.

2 Insert the knitting needle upwards through the yarn loop on your left thumb.

The thumb cast-on is a one-needle method that produces a flexible edge, which makes it particularly useful when using non-elastic yarns such as cotton. The 'give' in it also makes it a good one to use where the edge will turn back, as on the bootees with the blanket stitch detail (see page 56).

Unlike with two-needle methods, you are working towards the yarn end, which means you have to predict the length you need to cast on the required amount of stitches, otherwise you may find you do not have enough yarn to complete the last few stitches and have to start all over again. If unsure, always allow for more yarn than you think you need as you can use what is left over for sewing up.

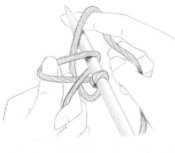

3 With the right index finger, wrap the yarn from the ball up and over the point of the knitting needle.

4 Draw the yarn through the loop on your thumb to form a new stitch on the knitting needle. Then, let the yarn loop slip off your left thumb and pull the loose end to tighten up the stitch. Repeat these steps until the required number of stitches have been cast on.

cable cast-on

1 Make a slip-knot as shown on page 15. Hold the knitting needle with the slip-knot in your left hand and insert the right-hand needle from left to right and from front to back through the slip-knot. Wrap the yarn from the ball up and over the point of the right-hand needle as shown.

2 With the right-hand needle, draw a loop through the slip-knot to make a new stitch. Do not drop the stitch from the left-hand needle, but instead slip the new stitch onto the left-hand needle as shown.

The cable cast-on method uses two needles and is particularly good for ribbed edges, as it provides a sturdy, but still elastic, edge. As you need to insert the needle between the stitches and pull the yarn through to create another stitch make sure that you do not make the new stitch too tight. The cable method is one of the most widely used cast-ons.

3 Next, insert the right-hand needle between the two stitches on the left-hand needle and wrap the yarn around the point of the right-hand needle.

4 Pull the yarn through to make a new stitch, and then place the new stitch on the left-hand needle, as before. Repeat the last two steps until the required number of stitches have been cast on.

knit & purl

The knit and purl stitches form the basis of almost all knitted fabrics. The knit stitch is the easiest to learn and is the first stitch you will create. When worked continuously it forms a reversible fabric called garter stitch. You can recognise garter stitch by the horizontal ridges formed at the top of the knitted loops.

After the knit stitch you will move on to the purl stitch. If you work the purl stitch continuously, it forms the same fabric as garter stitch. However, if you alternate the purl rows with knit rows, it creates stocking stitch, which is the most widely used knitted fabric.

knit

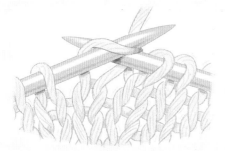 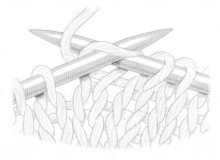 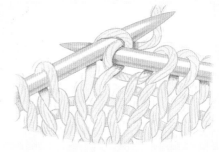

1 With the cast-on stitches on the needle in your left hand, insert the right-hand needle from left to right and from front to back through the first cast-on stitch.

2 Take the yarn from the ball on your index finger (the working yarn) around the point of the right-hand needle.

3 Draw the right-hand needle and yarn through the stitch, thus forming a new stitch on the right-hand needle, and at the same time slip the original stitch off the left-hand needle. Repeat these steps until all the stitches from the left-hand needle have been worked. One knit row has now been completed.

purl

  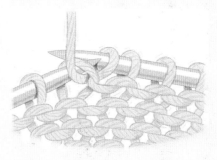

1 With the yarn to the front of the work, insert the right-hand needle from the right to the left into the front of the first stitch on the left-hand needle.

2 Then take the yarn from the ball on your index finger (the working yarn) around the point of the right-hand needle.

3 Draw the right-hand needle and the yarn through the stitch, thus forming a new stitch on the right-hand needle, and at the same time slip the original stitch off the left-hand needle. Repeat these steps until all the stitches have been worked. One purl row has now been completed.

increase

increase one ('kfb')

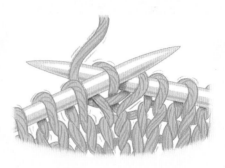

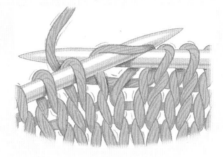

1 Insert the right-hand needle into the front of the next stitch, then knit the stitch but leave it on the left-hand needle.

2 Insert the right-hand needle into the back of the same stitch and knit it. Then slip the original stitch off the needle. Now you have made an extra stitch on the right-hand needle.

make one ('m1')

Increases are used to add to the width of the knitted fabric by creating more stitches. They are worked, for example, when shaping sleeves up the length of the arm or when additional stitches are needed after a ribbed welt. Some increases are invisible, while others are worked away from the edge of the work and are meant to be seen in order to give decorative detail. Most knitting patterns will tell you which type of increase to make.

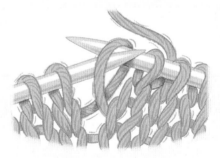

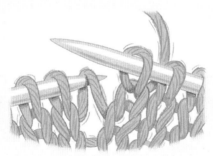

1 Insert the left-hand needle from front to back under the horizontal strand between the stitch just worked on the right-hand needle and the first stitch on the left-hand needle.

2 Knit into the back of the loop to twist it, and to prevent a hole. Drop the strand from the left-hand needle. This forms a new stitch on the right-hand needle.

yarn over

yarn over between knit stitches
Bring the yarn forward between the two needles, from the back to the front of the work. Taking the yarn over the right-hand needle to do so, knit the next stitch.

yarn over between purl stitches
Take the yarn over the right-hand needle to the back, then between the two needles to the front. Then purl the next stitch.

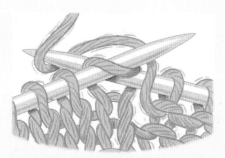

yarn over between a purl and a knit
Take the yarn from the front over the right-hand needle to the back. Then knit the next stitch.

yarn over between a knit and a purl
Bring the yarn forward between the two needles from the back to the front of the work, and take it over the top of the right-hand needle to the back again and then forward between the needles. Then purl the next stitch.

cast off

knit cast off

 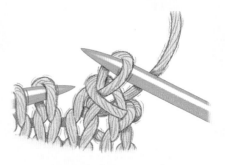

1 Knit two stitches. Insert the left-hand needle into the first stitch knitted on the right-hand needle and lift this stitch over the second stitch and off the right-hand needle.

2 One stitch is now on the right-hand needle. Knit the next stitch. Repeat the first step until all the stitches have been cast off. Pull the yarn through the last stitch to fasten off.

purl cast off

1 Purl two stitches. Insert the left-hand needle into the front of the first stitch worked on the right-hand needle and lift this stitch over the second stitch and off the right-hand needle.

2 One stitch is now on the right-hand needle. Purl the next stitch. Repeat the first step until all the stitches have been cast off. Pull the yarn through the last stitch to fasten off.

Cast off is used to finish off your knitted piece so that the stitches don't unravel. It is also used to decrease more than one stitch at a time, such as when shaping armholes, neckbands, and buttonholes. It is important that a cast off is firm but elastic, particularly when casting off around a neckband, to ensure that it can be pulled easily over the head. Unless told otherwise, cast off in the pattern used in the piece.

decrease

Decreases are used to make the fabric narrower by getting rid of stitches on the needle. They are worked to make an opening for a neckline or shaping a sleeve head. As with increases they can be used to create decorative detail, often around a neck edge. Increases and decreases are used together to create lace patterns.

knit 2 together

knit 2 together ('k2tog' or 'dec one')
On a knit row, insert the right-hand needle from left to right through the next two stitches on the left-hand needle and knit them together. One stitch has been decreased.

purl 2 together

purl 2 together ('p2tog' or 'dec one')
On a purl row, insert the right-hand needle from right to left through the next two stitches on the left-hand needle. Then purl them together. One stitch has been decreased.

slip stitch over

slip 1, knit 1, pass slipped stitch over ('psso')
1 Insert the right-hand needle into the next stitch on the left-hand needle and slip it onto the right-hand needle without knitting it. Knit the next stitch. Then insert the left-hand needle into the slipped stitch as shown.

2 With the left-hand needle, lift the slipped stitch over the knitted stitch as shown and off the right-hand needle.

reading patterns

To those unfamiliar with knitting patterns they can appear to be written in a strange, alien language! However as you become used to the terminology you will see that they have a logic and consistency that you will soon become familiar with.

Do not be too concerned if you read through a pattern first and are confused by parts of it as some instructions make more sense when your stitches are on the needle and you are at that point in the piece. However, it is sometimes a good idea to check with your retailer whether your skill levels are up to a particular design as this can prevent frustration later on.

Figures for larger sizes are given in round ( ) brackets. Where only one figure appears it means that those numbers apply to all sizes. Figures in square brackets [ ] are to be worked the number of times stated after the brackets. Where 0 appears, no stitches or rows are worked for this size.

When you follow the pattern it is important that you consistently use the right stitches or rows for your size, and you don't switch inside the brackets. This can be avoided by marking off your size throughout with a highlighting pen, but photocopy the pattern first so that you don't spoil your book.

Before starting your project check the size and the actual measurements that are quoted for that size, you may want to make a smaller or larger garment depending on the proportions of the wearer it is intended for.

The quantities of yarn quoted in the instructions are based on the yarn used by the knitter of the original garment and therefore all amounts should be considered approximate. For example, if that knitter has used almost all of the last ball, it may be that another knitter with a slightly different tension has to break into another ball to complete the garment. A slight variation in tension can therefore make the difference between using fewer or more balls than that stated in the pattern.

tension

Every knitting pattern will state a tension or gauge – the number of stitches and rows to 10cm that should be obtained with the quoted yarn, needle size and stitch pattern. It is vital to check your tension before starting your project. A slight variation can alter the proportions of the finished garment and the look of the fabric. A too loose tension will produce an uneven and unstable fabric that can drop or lose its shape after washing, whilst a too tight tension can make a hard, inelastic fabric.

Making a tension square

Use the same needles, yarn and stitch pattern quoted in the tension note in the pattern. Knit a sample at last 13cm square to get the most accurate result.

Smooth out the finished sample on a flat surface making sure you are not stretching it out. To check the stitch tension, place a tape measure or ruler horizontally on the sample and mark 10cm with pins. Count the number of stitches between the pins. To check the row tension, mark 10cm with pins vertically as before and count the number of rows. If the number of stitches and rows is greater than that quoted in the pattern, your tension is tighter and you should try changing to a larger needle and trying another tension square. If there are fewer stitches and rows, your tension is looser and you should try again on a smaller needle. The stitch tension is the most important to get right as the number of stitches in a pattern are set but the length is often calculated in measurement rather than rows and you may be able to work more or fewer rows.

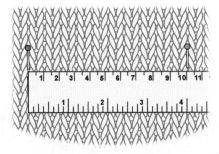

abbreviations

In a pattern book general abbreviations will usually be given at the front before the patterns begin, whilst those more specific to a particular design will be given at the start of the individual pattern. The following are the ones used throughout this book.

standard abbreviations

alt = alternate
beg = begin(ning)
cont = continue
dec = decrease (ing)
foll = following
garter st = garter stitch (k every row)
inc = increase (ing)
k = knit
kfb = knit into front and back of next st
m1 = make one stitch by picking up the loop lying between the stitch just worked and the next stitch and working into the back of it
patt = pattern
p = purl
psso = pass slipped stitch over
rem = remain (ing)
rep = repeat (ing)
skpo = slip 1, knit 1, pass slipped stitch over
sl = slip
ssk = [slip 1 knitwise] twice, insert tip of left-hand needle from left to right through slipped sts and k2tog
st(s) = stitch(es)
st st = stocking stitch
tbl = through back of loop
tog = together
yf = yarn forward
yon = yarn over needle
yrn = yarn round needle

cables

back cross 6 stitch cable ('C6B')

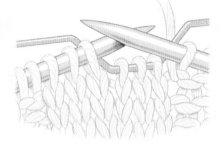
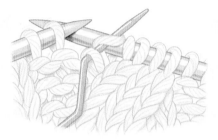

1 Slip the first three cable stitches purlwise off the left-hand needle and onto the cable needle. Leave the cable needle at the back of the work, then knit the next three stitches on the left-hand needle, keeping the yarn tight to prevent a gap from forming in the knitting.

2 Knit the three stitches directly from the cable needle, or if preferred, slip the three stitches from the cable needle back onto the left-hand needle and then knit them. This completes the cable cross.

front cross 6 stitch cable ('C6F')

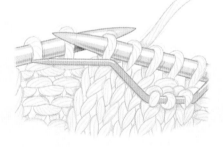

Cables are formed by the simple technique of crossing one set of stitches over another. Stitches are held on a cable needle (a short double-pointed needle) at the back or front of the work while the same amount of stitches is worked from the left-hand needle. Simple cables form a vertical twisted rope of stocking stitch on a background of reverse stocking stitch and tend to be worked over four or six stitches.

1 Slip the first three cable stitches purlwise off the left-hand needle and onto the cable needle. Leave the cable needle at the front of the work, then knit the next three stitches on the left-hand needle, keeping the yarn tight to prevent a gap from forming in the knitting.

2 Knit the three stitches directly from the cable needle, or if preferred, slip the three stitches from the cable needle back onto the left-hand needle and then knit them. This completes the cable cross.

intarsia

Intarsia is used when you are working with larger areas of usually isolated colour, such as when knitting motifs. If the yarn not in use was stranded or woven behind, it could show through to the front or pull in the colour work. In intarsia you use a separate strand or small ball of yarn for each colour area and then twist them together where they meet to prevent a gap forming.

vertical

rs

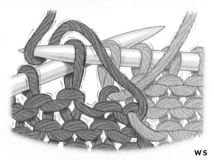

ws

right diagonal

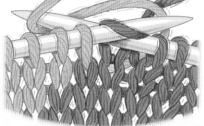

rs

ws

left diagonal

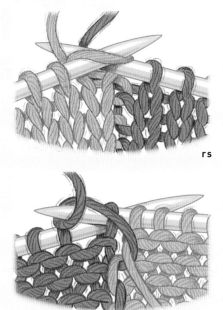

rs

ws

changing colours on a vertical line
If the two colour areas are forming a vertical line, to change colours on a knit row drop the colour you were using. Pick up the new colour and wrap it around the dropped colour as shown, then continue with the new colour. Twist the yarns together on knit and purl rows in this same way at vertical-line colour changes.

changing colours on a right diagonal
If the two colour areas are forming a right diagonal line, on a knit row drop the colour you were using. Pick up the new colour and wrap it around the dropped colour as shown, then continue with the new colour. Twist the yarns together on knit rows only at right-diagonal colour changes.

changing colours on a left diagonal
If the two colour areas are forming a left diagonal line, on a purl row drop the colour you were using. Pick up the new colour and wrap it around the colour just dropped as shown, then continue with the new colour. Twist the yarns together on purl rows only at left-diagonal colour changes.

reading charts

Most colour patterns are worked from a chart rather than set out in the text. Each square represents a stitch and row and the symbol or colour within it will tell you which colour to use. There will be a key listing the symbols used and the colour they represent.

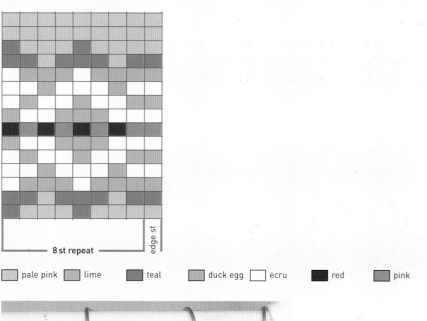

8 st repeat   edge st

☐ pale pink ☐ lime ■ teal ☐ duck egg ☐ ecru ■ red ■ pink

Unless stated otherwise, the first row of the chart is worked from right to left and represents the first right side row of your knitting. The second chart row represents the second and wrong side row and is read and worked from left to right.

If the colour pattern is a repeated design, as in Fairisle, the chart will tell you how many stitches are in each repeat. You will repeat these stitches as many times as is required. At each side of the repeat there may be edge stitches, these are only worked at the beginning and end of the rows and they indicate where you need to start and end for the piece you are knitting. Most colour patterns are worked in stocking stitch.

stranding

stranding on a knit row

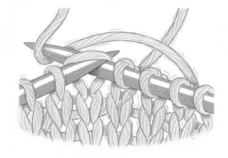 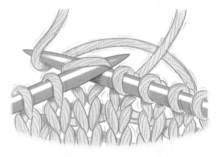

1 On a right-side (knit) row, to change colours drop the colour you were using. Pick up the new colour, take it over the top of the dropped colour and start knitting with it.

2 To change back to the old colour, drop the colour you were knitting with. Pick up the old colour, take it under the dropped colour and knit to the next colour change, and so on.

stranding on a purl row

Stranding is used when colour is worked over a small amount of stitches where using two colours in a row. The colour you are not using is left hanging on the wrong side of the work and then picked up when it is needed again. This creates strands at the back of the work called floats. Care must be taken so that they are not pulled too tightly as this will pucker the fabric. By picking up the yarns over and under one another you will prevent them tangling.

1 On a wrong-side (purl) row, to change colours drop the colour you were using. Pick up the new colour, take it over the top of the dropped colour and start purling with it.

2 To change back to the old colour, drop the colour you were knitting with. Pick up the old colour, take it under the dropped colour and purl to the next colour change, and so on.

&weaving in

weaving in on a knit row

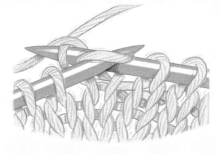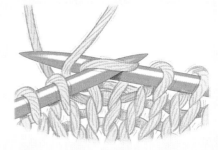

1 To weave in yarn on a knit stitch, insert the right-hand needle into the next stitch and lay the yarn to be woven in over the right-hand needle. Knit the stitch with the working yarn, taking it under the yarn not in use and making sure you do not catch this strand into the knitted stitch.

2 Knit the next stitch with the working yarn, taking it over the yarn being woven in. Continue like this, weaving the loose colour over and under the working yarn until you need to use it again.

weaving in on a purl row

When there are more than four stitches between a colour change, the floats are too long and this makes the fabric inflexible. The long strands can also catch when wearing the garment, particularly on the inside of a sleeve. By weaving in, the yarn not in use is caught up before the next colour change, thus shortening the float. Sometimes, depending on the colour pattern, a combination of both stranding and weaving can be used.

1 To weave in yarn on a purl stitch, insert the right-hand needle into the next stitch and lay the yarn to be woven in over the right-hand needle. Purl the stitch with the working yarn, taking it under the yarn not in use and making sure you do not catch this strand into the purled stitch.

2 Purl the next stitch with the working yarn, taking it over the yarn being woven in. Continue like this, weaving the loose colour over and under the working yarn until you need to use it again.

seaming

When you have completed the pieces of your knitting you reach one of the most important stages. The way you sew up or finish your project determines how good your finished garment will look. There are different types of seaming techniques but the best by far is mattress or ladder stitch, which creates an invisible seam. It can be used on stocking stitch, rib, garter and moss stitch.

The seam that I use for almost all sewing up is mattress stitch, which produces a wonderful invisible seam. It works well on any yarn, and makes a completely straight seam, as the same amount is taken up on each side – this also means that the knitted pieces should not need to be pinned together first. It is always worked on the right side of the fabric and is particularly useful for sewing up stripes and Fairisle.

I use other types of seams less frequently, but they do have their uses. For instance, backstitch can sometimes be useful for sewing in a sleeve head, to neatly ease in the fullness.

It is also good for catching in loose strands of yarn on colourwork seams, where there can be a lot of short ends along the selvedge. Just remember when using backstitch to sew up your knitting that it is important to ensure that you work in a completely straight line.

The seam for joining two cast-off edges is handy for shoulder seams, while the seam for joining a cast-off edge with a side edge (selvedge) is usually used when sewing a sleeve onto the body on a dropped shoulder style.

It is best to leave a long tail at the casting-on stage to sew up your knitting with, so that the sewing up yarn is already secured in place. If this

is not possible, when first securing the thread for the seam, you should leave a length that can be darned in afterwards. All seams on knitting should be sewn with a large blunt-tipped yarn or tapestry needle to avoid splitting the yarn.

Before sewing up side seams, join the shoulder seams and attach the sleeves, unless they are set-in sleeves. If there are any embellishments, such as applied pockets or embroidery, this is the time to put them on, when you can lay the garment out flat.

seams

**mattress stitch on stocking stitch
and double rib**
With the right sides of the knitting
facing you, insert the needle under the
horizontal bar between the first stitch
and next stitch. Then insert the needle
under the same bar on the other piece.
Continue to do this, drawing up the
thread to form the seam.

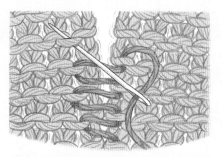

mattress stitch on garter stitch
With the right sides of the knitting
facing you, insert the needle through
the bottom of the 'knot' on the edge
and then through the top of the
corresponding 'knot' on the opposite
edge. Continue to do this from edge
to edge, drawing up the thread to
form a flat seam.

mattress stitch on moss stitch
With the right sides of the knitting
facing you, insert the needle under
the horizontal bar between the first
and second stitches on one side and
through the top of the 'knot' on the
edge of the opposite side.

joining two cast-off edges (grafting)
1 With the cast-off edges butted
together, bring the needle out in the
centre of the first stitch just below
the cast-off edge on one piece. Insert
the needle through the centre of the
first stitch on the other piece and out
through the centre of the next stitch.

2 Next, insert the needle through
the centre of the first stitch on the
first piece again and out through
the centre of the stitch next to it.
Continue in this way until the seam
is completed.

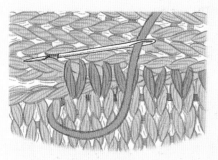

joining cast-off and selvedge edges
Bring the needle back to front through
the centre of the first stitch on the
cast-off edge. Then insert it under
one or two horizontal strands between
the first and second stitches on the
selvedge and back through the centre
of the same cast-off stitch. Continue in
this way until the seam is completed.

picking up stitches

When you are adding a border to your garment, such as front bands or a neckband, you usually pick up stitches around the edge. A border can be sewn on afterwards but this method is far neater. If you are picking up stitches along a long edge, a front band of a jacket for example, a long circular needle can be used so that you can fit all the stitches on. The pattern will usually tell you how many stitches to pick up.

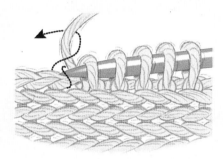

picking up stitches along a selvedge
With the right side of the knitting facing, insert the knitting needle from front to back between the first and second stitches of the first row. Wrap the yarn around the needle and pull a loop through to a form a new stitch on the needle. Continue in this way along the edge of the knitting.

picking up stitches along a neck edge
On a neck edge, work along the straight edges as for a selvedge. But along the curved edges, insert the needle through the centre of the stitch below the shaping (to avoid large gaps) and pull a loop of yarn through to form a new stitch on the needle.

patterns

blanket
with decorative edge

size
Approximately 46 x 69cm

materials
4 x 50g balls Debbie Bliss Baby Cashmerino in lilac (M)
1 x 50g ball Debbie Bliss Baby Cashmerino in each of silver (A) and chocolate (B)
Pair each 3.25mm and 3.75mm knitting needles

tension
25 sts and 44 rows to 10cm square over moss st using 3.25mm needles.

abbreviations
p2sso = pass 2 slipped sts over.
Also see page 25.

centre panel

With 3.25mm needles and M, cast on 97 sts.
Moss st row K1, [p1, k1] to end.
This row forms the moss st and is repeated throughout.
Cont in moss st until panel measures 62cm.
Cast off.

top & bottom edgings

With 3.75mm needles and B, cast on 127 sts.
Change to A.
1st row (right side) K1, skpo, k4, * skpo, sl 2tog, k3tog, p2sso, k2tog, k4; rep from * to last 16 sts, skpo, sl 2tog, k3tog, p2sso, k2tog, k4, k2tog, k1.
2nd row P7, * yrn, p1, yrn, p6; rep from * to last 8 sts, yrn, p1, yrn, p7.
3rd row K1, skpo, k1, yf, * k2, skpo, k1, k2tog, k2, yf; rep from * to last 4 sts, k1, k2tog, k1.
4th row P4, * yrn, p2, yrn, p3, yrn, p2, yrn, p1; rep from * to last 3 sts, p3.
5th row K1, skpo, k1, yf, k1, * yf, skpo, k1, sl 1, k2tog, psso, k1, k2tog, [yf, k1] 3 times; rep from * to last 14 sts, yf, skpo, k1, sl 1, k2tog, psso, k1, k2tog, [yf, k1] twice, k2tog, k1.
6th row P to end.
7th row K1, skpo, k3, * yf, sl 2tog, k3tog, p2sso, yf, k7; rep from * to last 11 sts, yf, sl 2tog, k3tog, p2sso, yf, k3, k2tog, k1.
K 3 rows. Cast off.

side edgings

With 3.75mm needles and B, cast on 205 sts.
Work as given for Top and Bottom Edgings.

to make up

Join corners of edging to form a square. Join cast-off edges of edging to centre section.

size
Approximately 45 x 71cm

materials
1 x 50g ball Debbie Bliss Baby Cashmerino in grey (A)
2 x 50g balls Debbie Bliss Baby Cashmerino in each of pale peach (B), silver (C) and ecru (D)
Pair 3.25mm knitting needles
3.25mm circular knitting needle

tension
25 sts and 50 rows to 10cm square over garter st using 3.25mm needles.

abbreviations
See page 25.

striped blanket

note
When working the stripe pattern in B, C and D, do not break off yarn but carry the colours not in use up the side edge, making sure not to pull too tightly or the blanket will be distorted.

to make
With 3.25mm needles and A, cast on 107 sts.
K 4 rows.
Break off yarn.
Cont in garter st and work in stripe sequence as follows: 2 rows C, 2 rows B, 2 rows D.
The last 6 rows form the striped pattern and are repeated throughout.
Cont in pattern until work measures 70cm from cast-on edge.
Change to A and k 4 rows.
Cast off.

side edgings
With 3.25mm circular needle and A, pick up and k117 sts along one side edge of blanket and k 4 rows.
Cast off.
Repeat on other side edge.

striped mouse

size
Approximately 18cm high

materials
Mouse 1 x 50g ball Debbie Bliss Baby Cashmerino in grey (A) and oddments of pale peach (B)
Pair 2.75mm knitting needles
Oddments of embroidery thread for eyes, snout and whiskers
Washable toy stuffing (see Note on opposite page)
Dress Oddments of Debbie Bliss Baby Cashmerino in grey (A), pale peach (B), silver (C) and ecru (D)
Pair 3.25mm knitting needles
Small button

tension
25 sts and 40 rows to 10cm square over st st using 2.75mm needles.

abbreviations
kfbf = knit into front, back and front of next st.
s2togkpo = slip 2 sts tog, k1, pass 2 slipped sts over.

note
Make sure you use a washable toy stuffing that is also non-flammable (flame retardant) and non-toxic and adheres to UK and EU safety regulations (BS5852, BS1425, EN71, PT2).

body

With 2.75mm needles and A, cast on 9 sts and p 1 row.
Next row (right side) [Kfb] 4 times, kfbf, [kfb] 4 times. 19 sts.
P 1 row.
Next row K5, m1, k1, m1, k8, m1, k1, m1, k4. 23 sts.
P 1 row.
Next row K6, m1, k1, m1, [k5, m1] twice, k1, m1, k5. 28 sts.
P 1 row.
Next row K14, m1, k1, m1, k13. 30 sts.
Beg with a p row, work 17 rows in st st.
Next row K5, k2tog, k1, ssk, k3, ssk, k1, k2tog, k3, k2tog, k1, ssk, k4. 24 sts.
P 1 row.
Next row K4, k2tog, k1, ssk, k2, ssk, k3, k2tog, k1, ssk, k3. 19 sts.
P 1 row.
Next row K3, k2tog, k1, ssk, k4, k2tog, k1, ssk, k2. 15 sts.
P 1 row.
Next row K2, k2tog, k1, ssk, k2, k2tog, k1, ssk, k1. 11 sts.
P 1 row.
Cast off.
Run a thread around the cast-off edge, pull up and join back seam, leaving a gap.
Stuff and close gap in seam.

head

With 2.75mm needles and A, cast on 4 sts and p 1 row.
Next row [Kfb] 3 times, k1. 7 sts.
P 1 row.
Next row K1, [m1, k2, m1, k1] to end. 11 sts.
Beg with a p row, work 3 rows in st st.
Next row K1, [m1, k3] 3 times, m1, k1.
P 1 row.
Next row K1, m1, k to last st, m1, k1.
Next row P1, m1, p to last st, m1, p1.
Next row K1, [m1, k3] twice, m1, k5, [m1, k3] twice, m1, k1. 25 sts.
Place markers at each end of last row.
Beg with a p row, work 6 rows.
Next row P4, p2tog, p13, p2tog tbl, p4.
Next row K14, ssk, turn.
Next row Sl 1, p5, p2tog, turn.
Next row Sl 1, k5, ssk, turn.
Rep last 2 rows 6 times more.
Cast off purlwise, working last 2 sts tog.
Join seam from point of snout to markers, and stuff head.

outer ears (make 2)

With 2.75mm needles and A, cast on 7 sts.
Beg with a k row, work 4 rows in st st.
Next row Ssk, k3, k2tog.
P 1 row.
Next row Ssk, k1, k2tog.
Next row P3tog and fasten off.

inner ears (make 2)

With 2.75mm needles and B, cast on 6 sts.
Beg with a k row, work 3 rows in st st.
Next row P2tog, p2, p2tog tbl.
Next row Ssk, k2tog.
Next row P3tog and fasten off.

arms (make 2)

With 2.75mm needles and A, cast on 4 sts and p 1 row.
Next row [Kfb] 3 times, k1. 7 sts.
P 1 row.
Next row [K1, m1, k2, m1] twice, k1. 11 sts.
Beg with a p row, work 3 rows in st st.
Next row K3, ssk, k1, k2tog, k3. 9 sts.
Beg with a p row, work 13 rows in st st.
Place markers at each end of last row.
Next row K1, ssk, k3, k2tog, k1. 7 sts.
P 1 row.
Next row K1, ssk, k1, k2tog, k1. 5 sts.
P 1 row.
Next row K1, s2togkpo, k1. 3 sts.
P 1 row.
Next row S2togkpo. 1 st.
Fasten off.
Join arm seam, from cast-on edge to markers, and stuff.

legs (make 2)

With 2.75mm needles and A, cast on 8 sts and p 1 row.
Next row (right side) [Kfb] 7 times, k1. 15 sts.
P 1 row.
Next row K1, m1, k4, [m1, k1] 6 times, k3, m1, k1. 23 sts.
Beg with a p row, work 3 rows in st st.
Next row K9, k2tog, k1, ssk, k9. 21 sts.
P 1 row.
Next row K8, k2tog, k1, ssk, k8. 19 sts.
Next row P7, p2tog tbl, p1, p2tog, p7. 17 sts.
Next row K7, s2togkpo, k7. 15 sts.
P 1 row.
Next row K5, ssk, k1, k2tog, k5. 13 sts.
Beg with a p row, work 23 rows in st st.

Next row K1, [ssk] twice, k3, [k2tog] twice, k1. 9 sts.
P 1 row.
Next row K1, ssk, k3, k2tog, k1. 7 sts.
Next row P1, p2tog, p1, p2tog tbl, p1.
Break yarn, thread through rem 5 sts, pull up and secure.
Join leg seam, leaving a gap for stuffing. Stuff foot and leg, then close gap in seam.

tail

With 2.75mm needles and A, cast on 25 sts.
Cast off.

to finish

Sew ears together in pairs of inner and outer ear pieces and sew to head. Using embroidery thread, work eyes, snout and whiskers. Sew head onto body, gathering slightly around neck edge. Sew arms in place around open edge. Sew on legs and tail.

dress

With 3.25mm needles and A, cast on 48 sts.
K 1 row.
* Change to C and k 2 rows.
Change to B and k 2 rows.
Change to D and k 2 rows.
Rep from * 3 times more.
Change to C and work as follows:
Next row (right side) K10, [k2tog] 14 times, k10. 34 sts.
Divide for front and back yokes
Next row (wrong side) K6 (for right back), cast off 4 sts (for armhole), with one st on needle after cast off, k next 13 sts (for front), cast off 4 sts (for armhole), k to end (for left back).
Change to B and work as follows:
On first set of 6 sts (left back), k 13 rows.
Cast off knitwise.
With right side facing, rejoin B to 14 sts of front, k 13 rows.
Cast off knitwise.
With right side facing, rejoin B to 6 sts of right back, k 13 rows.
Cast off knitwise and leave a long length of yarn.
With the length of yarn, make a small button loop on edge of right back.
Join back seam from cast-on edge to beg of yoke.
Sew button onto left back.

reversible
blanket

size
Approximately 100 x 100 cm

materials
13 x 50g balls Debbie Bliss Cashmerino Aran in each of stone (A) and blue (B)
1 x 50g ball Debbie Bliss Cashmerino Aran in chocolate (C) for blanket stitch detail
5mm circular knitting needle

tension
18 sts and 24 rows to 10cm square over st st using 5mm needles.

abbreviations
See page 25.

first side

With 5mm circular needle and A, cast on 175 sts.
Working back and forth in rows throughout, k 5 rows.
Work in patt as follows:
1st row (right side) K7, [p1, k7] to last 8 sts, p1, k7.
2nd row K3, p3, [k1, p1, k1, p5] to last 9 sts, k1, p1, k1, p3, k3.
3rd row K5, [p1, k3] to last 6 sts, p1, k5.
4th row K3, p1, [k1, p5, k1, p1] to last 3 sts, k3.
5th row K3, p1, [k7, p1] to last 3 sts, k3.
6th row As 4th row.
7th row As 3rd row.
8th row As 2nd row.
These 8 rows form the patt with garter st edging.
Cont in patt until work measures 98cm from cast-on edge, ending with a right side row.
K 5 rows.
Cast off.

second side

With 5mm circular needle and B, cast on 175 sts.
Working back and forth in rows throughout, k 5 rows.
Beg patt as follows:
1st row (right side) K3, [p1, k7] to last 4 sts, p1, k3.
2nd row K3, [p7, k1] to last 4 sts, p1, k3.
3rd row K5, [p1, k7] to last 10 sts, p1, k9.
4th row K3, p5, [k1, p7] to last 7 sts, k1, p3, k3.
5th row K7, [p1, k7] to end.
6th row K3, p3, [k1, p7] to last 9 sts, k1, p5, k3.
7th row K9, [p1, k7] to last 6 sts, p1, k5.
8th row K3, p1, [k1, p7] to last 3 sts, k3.
These 8 rows form the patt with garter st edging.
Cont in patt until work measures 98cm from cast-on edge, ending with a right side row.
K 5 rows.
Cast off.

to make up

With wrong sides together, join first and second sides together around the outer edge.

to finish

With two strands of C held together, work blanket stitch around the edges.

bootees
with blanket stitch detail

size
To fit ages 3–6 months

materials
1 x 50g ball Debbie Bliss Baby Cashmerino in pale blue (A) and oddments of chocolate (B) for blanket stitch detail
Pair 2.75mm knitting needles

tension
28 sts and 50 rows to 10cm square over garter st using 2.75mm needles.

abbreviations
See page 25.

boots (make 2)
With 2.75mm needles and A, cast on 36 sts.
K 36 rows.
Shape instep
Next row K23, turn.
Next row K10, turn.
Work 24 rows in garter st on centre 10 sts.
Next row K1, skpo, k to last 3 sts, k2tog, k1.
K 1 row.
Cut yarn.
With right side facing, rejoin yarn at base of instep and pick up and k13 sts along side of instep, k across centre 8 sts, then pick up and k13 sts along other side of instep. 34 sts.
Beg with a p row, work 5 rows in st st on these 34 sts.
Next row [K next st tog with corresponding st 5 rows below] 34 times, then k to end.
Next row K to end. 60 sts.
K 12 rows.
Beg with a k row, work 7 rows in st st.
Next row [P next st tog with corresponding st 7 rows below] to end.
Break off yarn.
Shape sole
Next row Slip first 25 sts onto right-hand needle, rejoin yarn and k10 sts, turn.
Next row K9, k2tog, turn.
Rep last row until 20 sts rem.
Cast off.

to finish
Join back seam. With back seam to centre of cast-off edge, join heel seam.
With B, work blanket stitch around edge of turnover.

rabbit
with blanket stitch detail

size
Approximately 25cm high

materials
2 x 50g balls Debbie Bliss Baby Cashmerino in pale blue (A), and oddments in each of chocolate (B) for embroidery and ecru (C) for pompon tail
Pair 2.75mm knitting needles
Washable toy stuffing (see Note on page 47)
10cm square of chocolate felt

tension
28 sts and 58 rows to 10cm square over garter st using 2.75mm needles.

abbreviations
ytb = yarn to back of work between two needles.
ytf = yarn to front of work between two needles.
s2togkpo = slip 2 sts tog, k1, pass 2 slipped sts over.
Also see page 25.

body back

(Worked from neck edge)
With 2.75mm needles and A, cast on 12 sts and k 1 row.
Shape shoulders
Next row [K2, m1] twice, k4, [m1, k2] twice. 16 sts.
K 1 row.
Next row K3, m1, k2, m1, k6, m1, k2, m1, k3. 20 sts.
K 5 rows.
Next row K1, m1, k to last st, m1, k1. 22 sts.
K 5 rows. **
Rep the last 6 rows 5 times more. 32 sts.
Shape base
Next row K1, [ssk, k11, k2tog] twice, k1. 28 sts.
K 1 row.
Next row K1, [ssk, k9, k2tog] twice, k1. 24 sts.
K 1 row.
*** **Next row** K1, [ssk, k7, k2tog] twice, k1. 20 sts.
K 1 row.
Cont to dec 4 sts in this way on every alt row until 8 sts rem.
Next row K1, sl 1, k2tog, psso, k3tog, k1. 4 sts.
Next row [K2tog] twice. 2 sts.
Next row K2tog and fasten off.

body front

Work as Body Back to **.
Next row K1, m1, k to last st, m1, k1. 24 sts.
K 5 rows.
Next row K1, m1, k10, m1, k2, m1, k10, m1, k1. 28 sts.
K 5 rows.
Next row K1, m1, k10, m1, k6, m1, k10, m1, k1. 32 sts.
K 5 rows.
Next row K1, m1, k to last st, m1, k1. 34 sts.
K 5 rows.
Rep the last 6 rows once more. 36 sts.
Next row K1, ssk, k6, [ssk, k5, k2tog] twice, k6, k2tog, k1. 30 sts.
K 1 row.
Next row K1, ssk, k5, [ssk, k3, k2tog] twice, k5, k2tog, k1. 24 sts.
K 1 row.
Now work as Body Back from *** to end.

head

With 2.75mm needles and A, cast on 4 sts.
1st row K.
2nd row K1, [m1, k1] to end. 7 sts.
Rep the last 2 rows once more. 13 sts.
5th, 7th, 9th and 11th rows K.
6th row [K1, m1, k5, m1] twice, k1. 17 sts.
8th row K1, m1, k6, m1, k3, m1, k6, m1, k1. 21 sts.
10th row K1, m1, k7, m1, k5, m1, k7, m1, k1. 25 sts.
12th row K1, m1, k8, m1, k7, m1, k8, m1, k1. 29 sts.
K 2 rows.
15th row K2, [ssk, k1] 3 times, k8, [k2tog, k1] 3 times, k1. 23 sts.
16th row K4, m1, k3, m1, k9, m1, k3, m1, k4. 27 sts.
K 3 rows.
20th row [K4, m1] twice, k11, [m1, k4] twice. 31 sts.
K 3 rows.
24th row K4, m1, k5, m1, k13, m1, k5, m1, k4. 35 sts.
K 1 row.
26th row K4, m1, k6, m1, k15, m1, k6, m1, k4. 39 sts.
K 1 row.
28th row K4, m1, k7, m1, k17, m1, k7, m1, k4. 43 sts.
K 1 row.
30th row K3, [m1, k4] 3 times, m1, k13, m1, [k4, m1] 3 times, k3. 51 sts.
K 12 rows.
43rd row K9, k2tog, [k8, k2tog] 4 times. 46 sts.
K 1 row.
45th row K8, k2tog, [k7, k2tog] 4 times. 41 sts.
K 1 row.
47th row K7, k2tog, [k6, k2tog] 4 times. 36 sts.
K 1 row.

Dec 5 sts in this way on next row and 4 foll alt rows. 11 sts.
K 1 row.
Next row Sl 1, k2tog, psso, [k2tog] 4 times. 5 sts.
Break yarn, thread through rem sts, pull up and secure.
Join seam, leaving a gap. Stuff carefully and close gap in seam.

ears (make 2)

With 2.75mm needles and A, cast on 15 sts.
K 1 row.
** Next 2 rows K2, ytf, sl 1, turn, ytf, sl 1, ytb, k2.
Next 2 rows K4, ytf, sl 1, turn, ytf, sl 1, ytb, k4.
Next 2 rows K6, ytf, sl 1, turn, ytf, sl 1, ytb, k6.
Next 2 rows K7, ytf, sl 1, turn, ytf, sl 1, ytb, k7.
K 1 row across all sts. **
Rep from ** to ** once more.
K 48 rows.
Next row K1, skpo, k to last 3 sts, k2tog, k1.
K 3 rows.
Rep the last 4 rows once more. 11 sts.
Next row K1, skpo, k to last 3 sts, k2tog, k1.
K 1 row.
Rep the last 2 rows twice more. 5 sts.
Next row K1, s2togkpo, k1.
Next row S2togkpo and fasten off.
Fold cast-on edge in half and join.
With B, work blanket st around edge of each ear.

legs (make 2)

With 2.75mm needles and A, cast on 15 sts.
K 1 row.
2nd row K1, m1, k4, m1, k1, m1, k3, m1, k1, m1, k4, m1, k1. 21 sts.
K 1 row.
4th row K1, m1, k6, m1, k2, m1, k3, m1, k2, m1, k6, m1, k1. 27 sts.
K 1 row.
6th row K9, m1, k3, [m1, k1] 3 times, m1, k3, m1, k9. 33 sts.
K 9 rows.
16th row K12, ssk, k5, k2tog, k12. 31 sts.
K 1 row.
18th row K12, ssk, k3, k2tog, k12. 29 sts.
K 1 row.
20th row K12, ssk, k1, k2tog, k12. 27 sts.
K 1 row.
22nd row K11, ssk, k1, k2tog, k11. 25 sts.
K 1 row.
24th row K10, ssk, k1, k2tog, k10. 23 sts.
K 1 row.

26th row K9, ssk, k1, k2tog, k9. 21 sts.
K 28 rows.
56th row K4, ssk, k9, k2tog, k4. 19 sts.
K 1 row.
58th row K4, ssk, k7, k2tog, k4. 17 sts.
K 1 row.
60th row K2, ssk, k2tog, k5, ssk, k2tog, k2. 13 sts.
K 1 row.
62nd row K1, ssk, k2tog, s2togkpo, ssk, k2tog, k1. 7 sts.
K 1 row.
64th row K1, ssk, k1, k2tog, k1. 5 sts.
Break yarn, thread through rem sts, pull up and secure.

arms (make 2)

With 2.75mm needles and A, cast on 7 sts.
K 1 row.
2nd row [K1, m1, k2, m1] twice, k1. 11 sts.
K 1 row.
4th row K1, m1, [k3, m1] 3 times, k1. 15 sts.
K 1 row.
6th row K1, m1, k4, m1, k5, m1, k4, m1, k1. 19 sts.
K 1 row.
8th row K1, m1, k17, m1, k1. 21 sts.
K 1 row.
10th row K1, m1, k7, ssk, k1, k2tog, k7, m1, k1. 21 sts.
K 1 row.
Rep the last 2 rows once more.
14th row K8, ssk, k1, k2tog, k8. 19 sts.
K 1 row.
16th row K7, ssk, k1, k2tog, k7. 17 sts.
K 24 rows.
41st row K2, ssk, k2tog, k5, ssk, k2tog, k2. 13 sts.
K 1 row.
43rd row K1, ssk, k2tog, s2togkpo, ssk, k2tog, k1. 7 sts.
K 1 row.
45th row K1, ssk, k1, k2tog, k1. 5 sts.
Break yarn, thread through rem sts, pull up and secure.

to make up

Join body back to body front leaving neck edge open. Stuff firmly and run a thread around neck edge, pull up slightly and secure. Sew ears to head. Embroider facial features with B. Sew head to body at neck. Fold each arm and each leg in half, join seam leaving a gap, stuff firmly and close gap. Sew arms and legs in place to body. Using the little bear sole template on page 120, cut two soles from chocolate felt and sew to feet. With B, work 'toes' and 'paws' on feet and arms. Make a small pompon in C and sew to body.

size
Approximately 76 x 97cm

materials
10 x 50g balls Debbie Bliss Cashmerino Aran in each of charcoal grey (A) and mid grey (B)
1 x 50g ball Debbie Bliss Cashmerino Aran in silver (C)
5mm circular knitting needle

tension
20 sts and 26 rows to 10cm square over patt using 5mm needles.

abbreviations
See page 25.

running stitch blanket

first side

With 5mm circular needle and A, cast on 151 sts.
1st row K1, [p1, k3] to last 2 sts, p1, k1.
2nd row Purl.
These 2 rows form the broken rib patt and are repeated throughout.
Cont in patt until work measures approximately 97cm, ending with a 1st row, making sure you have enough yarn for casting off and sewing up.
Cast off knitwise.

second side

Make exactly as for First Side, but using B.

to finish

Work contrast 'running stitch' in C on both pieces of blanket using the vertical lines as a guide and running the yarn under every alternate purl st. With wrong sides together, join first and second sides together, over-sewing with A around the outer edge.

size
Approximately 57 x 75cm

materials
5 x 50g balls Debbie Bliss Baby Cashmerino in silver (M)
1 x 50g ball Debbie Bliss Baby Cashmerino in each of camel (A) and stone (B)
Oddments of chocolate yarn (C) for embroidery
3.25mm circular knitting needle

tension
25 sts and 34 rows to 10cm square over st st using 3.25mm needles.

abbreviations
See page 25.

teddy blanket

to make

With 3.25mm circular needle and M, cast on 144 sts.
K 9 rows.
First line of motifs
1st row (right side) K39, [p1, k1] 16 times, p1, k33, [p1, k1] 16 times, p1, k6.
2nd row K6, [p1, k1] 16 times, p35, [k1, p1] 15 times, k1, p34, k6.
3rd to 9th rows Rep the 1st and 2nd rows 3 times more and the 1st row again.
10th row (wrong side) K6, [p1, k1] 16 times, p8, work across 1st row of Chart on page 71 (reading this chart row – a wrong side row – from left to right), p8, [k1, p1] 15 times, k1, p8, work across 1st row of Chart, p7, k6.
11th row K13, work across 2nd row of Chart (reading this chart row – a right side row – from right to left), k7, [p1, k1] 16 times, p1, k7, work across 2nd row of Chart, k7, [p1, k1] 16 times, p1, k6.
Working correct Chart rows, rep the last 2 rows 10 times more, so completing the Chart.
32nd row K6, [p1, k1] 16 times, p35, [k1, p1] 15 times, k1, p34, k6.
33rd to 40th rows Rep 1st and 2nd rows 4 times.
Second line of motifs
1st row (right side) K6, [p1, k1] 16 times, p1, k33, p1, [k1, p1] 16 times, k39.
2nd row K6, p34, [k1, p1] 15 times, k1, p35, [k1, p1] 16 times, k6.
3rd to 9th rows Rep the 1st and 2nd rows 3 times more and the first row again.

10th row (wrong side) K6, p7, work across 1st row of Chart, p8, [k1, p1] 15 times, k1, p8, work across 1st row of Chart, p8, [k1, p1] 16 times, k6.

11th row K6, [p1, k1] 16 times, p1, k7, work across 2nd row of Chart, k7, [p1, k1] 16 times, p1, k7, work across 2nd row of Chart, k13.

Working correct Chart rows, rep the last 2 rows 10 times more, so completing the Chart.

32nd row K6, p34, [k1, p1] 15 times, k1, p35, [k1, p1] 16 times, k6.

33rd to 40th rows Rep 1st and 2nd rows 4 times.

Third to sixth lines of motifs

Rep 1st and 2nd lines twice more.

K 10 rows.

Cast off.

to finish

With C, embroider features, using straight stitches.

teddy blanket chart

- When working from Chart, use a separate small ball of yarn for each colour area and twist yarns at colour change to avoid holes.
- Use A and B for bear motifs in alternate squares.

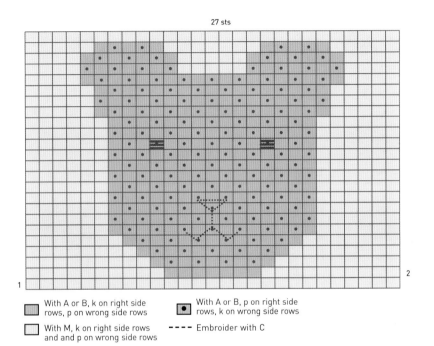

27 sts

	With A or B, k on right side rows, p on wrong side rows		With A or B, p on right side rows, k on wrong side rows
	With M, k on right side rows and and p on wrong side rows	- - - -	Embroider with C

teddy slippers chart

Read right side rows from right to left and wrong side rows from left to right. When working from chart use a separate ball of yarn for each colour area and twist yarns at colour change on wrong side to avoid a hole.

With M, p on right side rows, k on wrong side rows

With M, k on right side rows, p on wrong side rows

With A, k on right side rows, p on wrong side rows

With A, p on right side rows, k on wrong side rows

Embroider with C - - - -

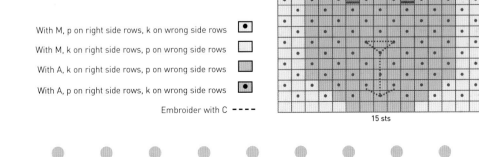

15 sts

size
To fit ages 3–6 months

materials
1 x 50g ball Debbie Bliss Baby Cashmerino in each of silver (M) and camel (A)
Oddments of chocolate yarn (B) for embroidery
Pair 2.75mm knitting needles

tension
27 sts and 46 rows to 10cm square over moss st using 2.75mm needles.

abbreviations
See page 25.

teddy slippers

to make

With 2.75mm needles and M, cast on 31 sts.
1st row (wrong side) P1, [k1, p1] to end.
This row **sets** the moss st.
Next row Work 2 tog, moss st to end.
Rep the last row 23 times more. 7 sts.
Next row Inc in first st, moss st to end.
Rep the last row 9 times more. 17 sts.
Next row (right side) Inc in first st, work across 1st row of Chart on page 71 (reading this chart row – a right side row – from right to left), moss st last st.
Next row Inc in first st, work across 2nd row of Chart (reading this chart row – a wrong side row – from left to right), moss st 2.
These 2 rows set the position of the Chart.
Cont in moss st with chart and inc one st at beg of next 12 rows. 31 sts.
Next row Work 2 tog, moss st to end.
Rep the last row 27 times more. 3 sts.
Cast off.

to finish

Embroider eyes, nose and mouth with B.
Fold cast-off edge and two corners into centre, and join seams.
Bring both ends of edging to centre, and join seams.

triangle edge top

measurements
To fit ages 3–6 (6–9: 9–12: 12–18) months
actual measurements
Chest 51 (56: 60: 65)cm
Length to shoulder 24 (26: 28: 32)cm
Sleeve length 15 (17: 19: 22)cm

materials
3 (4: 4: 5) x 50g balls Debbie Bliss Baby Cashmerino in lilac (M) and
oddments of aubergine (C) for edging
Pair each 3mm and 3.25mm knitting needles
One 3.25mm double-pointed knitting needle
3 buttons

tension
25 sts and 34 rows to 10cm square over st st using 3.25mm needles.

abbreviations
See page 25.

back

With 3mm needles and M, cast on 92 (98: 104: 110) sts.
Next row (wrong side) K to end.
Next row K39 (42: 45: 48), sl 1, k12, sl 1, k39 (42: 45: 48).
Next row K32 (35: 38: 41), sl 1, k26, sl 1, k32 (35: 38: 41).
Rep the last 2 rows twice more.
Change to 3.25mm needles.
Next row (right side) K39 (42: 45: 48), sl 1, k12, sl 1, k39 (42: 45: 48).
Next row P32 (35: 38: 41), sl 1, p26, sl 1, p32 (35: 38: 41).
Rep the last 2 rows until back measures 14 (15: 16: 19)cm, ending with a wrong side row.
Shape armholes
Cast off 4 sts at beg of next 2 rows. 84 (90: 96: 102) sts.
Work a further 14 rows.
Next row (right side) K29 (32: 35: 38), cast off 26, k to end. 58 (64: 70: 76) sts.
Cont straight until back measures 24 (26: 28: 32)cm, ending with a wrong side row.
Shape shoulders
Cast off 7 (8: 9: 10) sts at beg of next 4 rows.
Leave rem 30 (32: 34: 36) sts on a spare needle.

front

With 3mm needles and M, cast on 66 (72: 78: 84) sts.
K 7 rows.
Beg with a k row, work in st st until front measures 14 (15: 16: 19)cm, ending with a wrong side row.
Shape armholes
Cast off 4 sts at beg of next 2 rows. 58 (64: 70: 76) sts.
Front opening
Next row (right side) K29 (32: 35: 38), turn and cast on 4 sts, work on these 33 (36: 39: 42) sts for first side of front opening.
1st row K2, p to end.
2nd row K to end.
Rep the last 2 rows 10 times more and the first row again.
Shape neck
Next row (right side) K to last 11 (12: 13: 14) sts, leave these sts on a holder, turn and work on rem 22 (24: 26: 28) sts.
Dec 1 st at neck edge on every row until 14 (16: 18: 20) sts rem.
Work straight until front measures the same as Back to shoulder, ending at armhole edge.
Shape shoulder
Cast off 7 (8: 9: 10) sts at beg of next row.
Work 1 row.
Cast off rem 7 (8: 9: 10) sts.
With right side facing, rejoin yarn to rem 29 (32: 35: 38) sts.
1st row K to end.
2nd row P26 (29: 32: 33), k2, m1, k to end.
3rd to 6th rows Rep 1st and 2nd rows twice more.
7th row (buttonhole row) K2, k2tog, yf, k to end.
8th row P26 (29: 32: 33), k2, k into front and back of yf, k3.

9th and 10th rows As 1st and 2nd rows.
11th row Cast off 5 sts, k to end.
Rep 2nd to 11th rows once more then 2nd to 4th rows again.
Shape neck
Next row (right side) K9 (10: 11: 12), leave these sts on a holder, k to end.
Dec 1 st at neck edge on every row until 14 (16: 18: 20) sts rem.
Work straight until front measures same as Back to shoulder, ending at armhole edge.
Shape shoulder
Cast off 7 (8: 9: 10) sts at beg of next row.
Work 1 row.
Cast off rem 7 (8: 9: 10) sts.

sleeves

With 3mm needles and M, cast on 35 (37: 41: 43) sts.
K 7 rows.
Change to 3.25mm needles.
Beg with a k row, work in st st.
Work 2 rows.
Inc row K3, m1, k to last 3 sts, m1, k3.
Work 5 rows.
Rep the last 6 rows 5 (6: 7: 9) times more and the inc row again. 49 (53: 59: 65) sts.
Cont straight until sleeve measures 15 (17: 19: 22)cm, ending with a wrong side row.
Place markers at each end of last row.
Work a further 6 rows.
Cast off.

neckband

Join shoulder seams.
With right side facing, 3mm needles and M, slip 9 (10: 11: 12) sts from right front holder onto a needle, pick up and k12 (13: 14: 15) sts up right front neck, k30 (32: 34: 36) sts from back neck holder, pick up and k12 (13: 14: 15) sts down left front neck, then k11 (12: 13: 14) sts from left front holder. 74 (80: 86: 92) sts.
Next row (wrong side) K to last 3 sts, m1, k3.
Next row (buttonhole row) K2, k2tog, yf, k to end.
Next row K to last 4 sts, k into front and back of yf, k3.
Next row K to end.
Next row K to last 5 sts, m1, k5.
Cast off.

front edging

Cut a 2m length of contrast yarn (C).
With right side facing and using 3.25mm double-pointed needle, starting halfway along length of yarn, pick up and k6 sts along row ends of first point, * slip sts to other end of needle, using other half of yarn, cast off 5 sts, with one st on needle, use double-pointed needle and first half of yarn, pick up and k5 sts along cast-off edge of point, slip sts to other end of needle, using other half of yarn **, cast off 5 sts, with one st on needle, pick up and k5 sts along row ends of next point; rep from * once more, then from * to **, cast off rem 6 sts.

to make up

Matching centre of cast-off edge of sleeve to shoulder, sew sleeves into armholes, with row ends above markers sewn to sts cast off at underarm. Join side and sleeve seams. Sew cast-on sts for button band behind buttonhole band. Sew on buttons. Fold cast-off sts at centre back to form a box pleat on wrong side of work, and sew in place.

size
To fit ages 3–6 months

materials
1 x 50g ball Debbie Bliss Baby Cashmerino in lilac (M) and oddments of aubergine (C) for edging
Pair 2.75mm knitting needles
One 2.75mm double-pointed knitting needle

tension
25 sts and 34 rows to 10cm square over st st using 3.25mm needles.

abbreviations
See page 25.

triangle edge bootees

to make

With 2.75mm needles and M, cast on 36 sts.

K 1 row.

1st row (right side) K1, yf, k16, yf, [k1, yf] twice, k16, yf, k1.

2nd and all wrong side rows K to end, working k1 tbl into each yf of previous row.

3rd row K2, yf, k16, yf, k2, yf, k3, yf, k16, yf, k2.

5th row K3, yf, k16, yf, [k4, yf] twice, k16, yf, k3.

7th row K4, yf, k16, yf, k5, yf, k6, yf, k16, yf, k4.

9th row K5, yf, k16, yf, [k7, yf] twice, k16, yf, k5.

11th row K22, yf, k8, yf, k9, yf, k22. 64 sts.

12th row As 2nd row.

Beg with a k row, work 9 rows st st.

K 3 rows.

Shape instep

Next row K36, skpo, turn.

Next row Sl 1, p8, p2tog, turn.

Next row Sl 1, k8, skpo, turn.

Rep the last 2 rows 7 times more, then work first of the 2 rows again.

Next row Sl 1, k to end.

Next row P17, p2tog tbl, p8, p2tog, p17. 44 sts.

Dec row [K3, k2tog] 4 times, k4, [skpo, k3] 4 times. 36 sts.

Beg with a p row, work 15 rows in st st.

K 6 rows.

Cast off.

edging

With 2.75mm needles and M, cast on 3 sts.

1st row K2, m1, k to end.

2nd row K to end.

3rd to 9th rows Rep 1st and 2nd rows 3 times more and the first row again. 8 sts.

10th row Cast off 5 sts, k to end.

Rep 1st to 10th rows 5 times more, then 1st to 9th rows once more.

Cast off all sts.

Cut a 3m length of contrast yarn (C).

With right side facing and using 2.75mm double-pointed needle, starting halfway along length of yarn, pick up and k6 sts along row ends of first point, * slip sts to other end of needle, using other half of yarn, cast off 5 sts, with one st on needle, use double-pointed needle and first half of yarn pick up and k5 sts along cast-off edge of point, slip sts to other end of needle, using other half of yarn ** , cast off 5 sts, with one st on needle, pick up and k5 sts along row ends of next point; rep from * 5 times more, then from * to **, cast off rem 6 sts.

to make up

Join edging to cast-off sts of bootee. Join back and sole seam. Fold edging to right side.

size
Approximately 66 x 66cm

materials
10 x 50g balls Debbie Bliss Cashmerino Aran in ecru
Pair 5mm knitting needles
5mm circular knitting needle

tension
18 sts and 36 rows to 10cm square over garter st using 5mm needles.

abbreviations
See page 25.

hooded blanket

main part

With 5mm circular needle, cast on 3 sts and k 1 row.
Next row (right side) [K1, m1] twice, k1.
Next row K5.
Next row K2, m1, k1, m1, k2.
Next row K to end.
Next row K2, m1, k to last 2 sts, m1, k2.
Rep the last 2 rows until side edge measures 66cm, ending with a wrong side row.
Next row K1, skpo, k to last 3 sts, k2tog, k1.
Next row K to end.
Rep the last 2 rows until 5 sts rem, ending with a wrong side row.
Next row K1, s1 1, k2tog, psso, k1.
Cast off rem 3 sts.

hood

With 5mm needles, cast on 75 sts and k 1 row.
Next row (right side) K1, skpo, k to last 3 sts, k2tog, k1.
Next row K to end.
Rep the last 2 rows until 5 sts rem, ending with a wrong side row.
Next row K1, s1 1, k2tog, psso, k1.
Cast off rem 3 sts.

to make up

Sew hood to corner of main part.

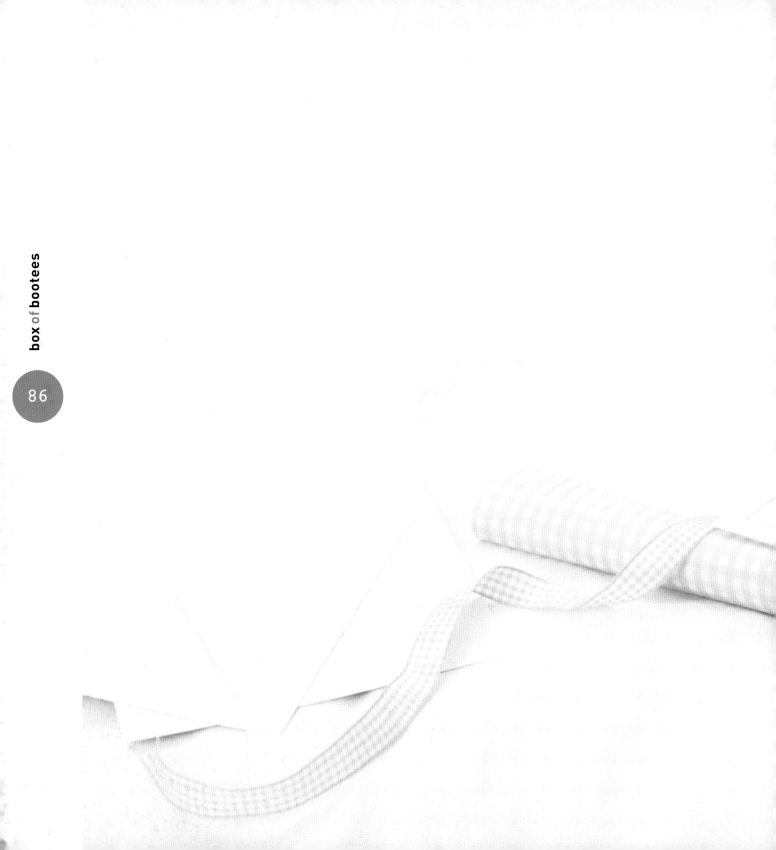

size
To fit age 3–6 months

materials
1 x 50g ball Debbie Bliss Baby Cashmerino in pale blue
Pair 2.75mm knitting needles
2 buttons

tension
28 sts and 37 rows to 10cm square over st st using 2.75mm needles.

abbreviations
See page 25.

sandals

right sandal

With 2.75mm needles, cast on 36 sts.

K 1 row.

1st row (right side) K1, yf, k16, yf, [k1, yf] twice, k16, yf, k1.

2nd and all wrong side rows K to end, working k1 tbl into each yf of previous row.

3rd row K2, yf, k16, yf, k2, yf, k3, yf, k16, yf, k2.

5th row K3, yf, k16, yf, [k4, yf] twice, k16, yf, k3.

7th row K4, yf, k16, yf, k5, yf, k6, yf, k16, yf, k4.

9th row K5, yf, k16, yf, [k7, yf] twice, k16, yf, k5.

11th row K22, yf, k8, yf, k9, yf, k22. 64 sts.

12th row As 2nd row.

Beg with a k row, work 7 rows in st st.

Next row [P next st tog with corresponding st 7 rows below] to end.

Beg with a k row, work 8 rows in st st.

Shape instep

Next row K36, skpo, turn.

Next row Sl 1, p8, p2tog, turn.

Next row Sl 1, k8, skpo, turn.

Rep the last 2 rows 7 times more, then work the first of the 2 rows again.

Next row Sl 1, k to end.

Next row K17, k2tog, p8, skpo, k17. 44 sts.

Next row K24, turn.

Next row P4, turn.

Next row K4, turn.

Work 6cm in st st on these 4 sts only for front strap.

Cast off these 4 sts.

With right side facing, rejoin yarn at base of strap, pick up and k15 sts along side edge of strap, then turn and cast off 26 sts knitwise, leave rem 9 sts on a holder.

With right side facing, rejoin yarn to top of other side of strap, pick up and k15 sts along side edge of strap, then k rem 20 sts.

Next row K9, cast off rem 26 sts knitwise.

Join sole and back heel seam.

With right side facing and 2.75mm needles, k across 18 sts along heel for ankle strap. **

Next row Cast on 22 sts, k to end, turn and cast on 4 sts.

Buttonhole row K to last 3 sts, yf, k2tog, k1.

K 2 rows.

Cast off.

Fold front strap over ankle strap and slip stitch cast-off edge in place.

Sew on button.

left sandal

Work as given for Right Sandal to **.

Next row Cast on 4 sts, k to end, turn and cast on 22 sts.

Buttonhole row K1, skpo, yf, k to end.

Complete as Right Sandal.

picot bootees

size
To fit age 3–6 months

materials
1 x 50g ball Debbie Bliss Baby Cashmerino in ecru
Pair 2.75mm knitting needles
2 buttons

tension
28 sts and 37 rows to 10cm square over st st using 2.75mm needles.

abbreviations
See page 25.

right bootee

With 2.75mm needles, cast on 36 sts.
K 1 row.
1st row (right side) K1, yf, k16, yf, [k1, yf] twice, k16, yf, k1.
2nd and all wrong side rows K to end, working k1 tbl into each yf of previous row.
3rd row K2, yf, k16, yf, k2, yf, k3, yf, k16, yf, k2.
5th row K3, yf, k16, yf, [k4, yf] twice, k16, yf, k3.
7th row K4, yf, k16, yf, k5, yf, k6, yf, k16, yf, k4.
9th row K5, yf, k16, yf, [k7, yf] twice, k16, yf, k5.
11th row K22, yf, k8, yf, k9, yf, k22. 64 sts.
12th row As 2nd row.
K 12 rows.
Shape instep
Next row K36, skpo, turn.
Next row Sl 1, p8, p2tog, turn.
Next row Sl 1, k8, skpo, turn.
Rep the last 2 rows 5 times more, then work first of the 2 rows again.
Next row Sl 1, k to end.
Next row K19, k2tog, k8, skpo, k19. 48 sts.
Next row K9, leave these sts on a holder, cast off one st, [slip the st now on right-hand needle back onto left-hand needle, cast on 2 sts, cast off 4 sts] 14 times, slip the st back onto left-hand needle, cast on 2 sts, cast off 3 sts, k to end, leave these 9 sts on a holder.
Join sole and back heel seam.
With wrong side facing and 2.75mm needles, k across 18 sts on holder for ankle strap. **
Next row Cast on 4 sts, k to end, turn and cast on 22 sts.
Buttonhole row K1, skpo, yf, k to end.
K 2 rows.
Cast off.
Sew on button.

left bootee

Work as given for Right Bootee to **.
Next row Cast on 22 sts, k to end, turn and cast on 4 sts.
Buttonhole row K to last 3 sts, yf, k2tog, k1.
Complete as Right Bootee.

size
To fit age 3–6 months

materials
1 x 50g ball Debbie Bliss Baby Cashmerino in teal
Pair 2.75mm knitting needles

tension
28 sts and 50 rows to 10cm square over garter st using 2.75mm needles.

abbreviations
See page 25.

baby bootees

to make

With 2.75mm needles, cast on 18 sts (for first half of cuff) and k 12 rows.
Break off yarn and leave these sts on a holder.
With 2.75mm needles, cast on 18 sts (for second half of cuff) and k 12 rows.
Join cuff halves
Next row [K1, p1] 9 times, then [k1, p1] 9 times across first half of cuff on holder. 36 sts.
Next row [K1, p1] to end.
Rep the last row 6 times more.
Shape instep
Next row (RS) K33, turn.
Next row K10, turn.
Work 24 rows in garter st on centre 10 sts.
Next row K1, skpo, k4, k2tog, k1. 8 sts.
K 1 row.
Cut yarn.
With RS facing, rejoin yarn at base of instep, pick up and k13 sts evenly along side of instep, k across centre 8 sts, then pick up and k13 sts evenly along other side of instep, k rem 13 sts. 60 sts.
K 13 rows.
Beg with a k row, work 7 rows in st st.
Next row [P next st tog with corresponding st 7 rows below] to end.
Break off yarn.
Shape sole
Next row Slip first 25 sts onto right-hand needle, rejoin yarn and k10 sts, turn.
Next row K9, k2tog, turn.
Rep last row until 20 sts rem.
Cast off.

to make up

Join back seam. With back seam to centre of cast off, join heel seam.

size
Approximately 90 x 110cm

materials
15 x 50g balls Debbie Bliss Baby Cashmerino in ecru (M)
Oddments of contrast yarn (C) for embroidery
3mm and 3.25mm circular knitting needles
Cable needle

tension
25 sts and 34 rows to 10cm square over st st using 3.25mm needles.

sampler blanket

abbreviations

C4B = slip next 2 sts onto cable needle and hold at back of work, k2, then k2 from cable needle.

C4F = slip next 2 sts onto cable needle and hold at front of work, k2, then k2 from cable needle.

C5F = slip next 3 sts onto cable needle and hold at front of work, k2, then slip the p st from cable needle back onto left-hand needle, p this st, then k2 from cable needle.

C6B = slip next 3 sts onto cable needle and hold at back of work, k3, then k3 from cable needle.

C6F = slip next 3 sts onto cable needle and hold at front of work, k3, then k3 from cable needle.

C3BP = slip next st onto cable needle and hold at back of work, k2, then p1 from cable needle.

C3FP = slip next 2 sts onto cable needle and hold at front of work, p1, then k2 from cable needle.

C4BP = slip next 2 sts onto cable needle and hold at back of work, k2, then p2 from cable needle.

C4FP = slip next 2 sts onto cable needle and hold at front of work, p2, then k2 from cable needle.

C5BP = slip next 2 sts onto cable needle and hold at back of work, k3, then p2 from cable needle.

C5FP = slip next 3 sts onto cable needle and hold at front of work, p2, then k3 from cable needle.

T5L = slip next 2 sts onto cable needle and hold at front of work, k2, p1, then k2 from cable needle.

MB = k into front, back and front of next st, [turn and k3] 3 times, turn and sl 1, k2tog, psso.

Also see page 25.

motif A
(worked over 40 sts)

1st row (right side) P9, T5L, p12, T5L, p9.
2nd row K9, p2, k1, p2, k12, p2, k1, p2, k9.
3rd row P8, C3BP, k1, C3FP, p10, C3BP, k1, C3FP, p8.
4th row K8, p2, k1, p1, k1, p2, k10, p2, k1, p1, k1, p2, k8.
5th row P7, C3BP, k1, p1, k1, C3FP, p8, C3BP, k1, p1, k1, C3FP, p7.
6th row K7, p2, [k1, p1] twice, k1, p2, k8, p2, [k1, p1] twice, k1, p2, k7.
7th row P6, C3BP, [k1, p1] twice, k1, C3FP, p6, C3BP, [k1, p1] twice, k1, C3FP, p6.
8th row K6, p2, [k1, p1] 3 times, k1, p2, k6, p2, [k1, p1] 3 times, k1, p2, k6.
9th row P5, C3BP, [k1, p1] 3 times, k1, C3FP, p4, C3BP, [k1, p1] 3 times, k1, C3FP, p5.
10th row K5, p2, [k1, p1] 4 times, k1, p2, k4, p2, [k1, p1] 4 times, k1, p2, k5.
11th row P4, C3BP, [k1, p1] 4 times, k1, C3FP, p2, C3BP, [k1, p1] 4 times, k1, C3FP, p4.
12th row K4, p2, [k1, p1] 5 times, k1, p2, k2, p2, [k1, p1] 5 times, k1, p2, k4.
13th to 36th rows Rep 1st to 12th rows twice more.
37th row P4, k3, [p1, k1] 4 times, p1, k3, p2, k3, [p1, k1] 4 times, p1, k3, p4.
38th row K4, p3, [k1, p1] 4 times, k1, p3, k2, p3, [k1, p1] 4 times, k1, p3, k4.

motif B
(worked over 40 sts)

1st row (right side) P9, C3BP, p5, C6B, p5, C3FP, p9.
2nd row K9, p2, k6, p6, k6, p2, k9.
3rd row P8, C3BP, p4, C5BP, C5FP, p4, C3FP, p8.
4th row K8, p2, k5, p3, k4, p3, k5, p2, k8.
5th row P7, C3BP, p3, C5BP, p4, C5FP, p3, C3FP, p7.
6th row K7, p2, k1, MB, k2, p3, k8, p3, k2, MB, k1, p2, k7.
7th row P7, C3FP, p3, k3, p8, k3, p3, C3BP, p7.
8th row K8, p2, k3, p3, k8, p3, k3, p2, k8.

9th row P8, C3FP, p2, C5FP, p4, C5BP, p2, C3BP, p8.

10th row K9, p2, [k4, p3] twice, k4, p2, k9.

11th row P9, C3FP, p3, C5FP, C5BP, p3, C3BP, p9.

12th row K8, MB, k1, p2, k5, p6, k5, p2, k1, MB, k8.

13th to 38th rows Rep 1st to 12th twice more, then 1st and 2nd rows again.

motif C
(worked over 40 sts)

1st row (right side) P10, C5F, p10, C5F, p10.

2nd row K10, p2, k1, p2, k10, p2, k1, p2, k10.

3rd row P9, C3BP, k1, C3FP, p8, C3BP, k1, C3FP, p9.

4th row K9, p2, k1, p1, k1, p2, k8, p2, k1, p1, k1, p2, k9.

5th row P8, C3BP, k1, p1, k1, C3FP, p6, C3BP, k1, p1, k1, C3FP, p8.

6th row K8, p2, [k1, p1] twice, k1, p2, k6, p2, [k1, p1] twice, k1, p2, k8.

7th row P7, C3BP, [k1, p1] twice, k1, C3FP, p4, C3BP, [k1, p1] twice, k1, C3FP, p7.

8th row K7, p2, [k1, p1] 3 times, k1, p2, k4, p2, [k1, p1] 3 times, k1, p2, k7.

9th row P6, C3BP, [k1, p1] 3 times, k1, C3FP, p2, C3BP, [k1, p1] 3 times, k1, C3FP, p6.

10th row K6, p2, [k1, p1] 4 times, k1, p2, k2, p2, [k1, p1] 4 times, k1, p2, k6.

11th row P6, C3FP, [p1, k1] 3 times, p1, C3BP, p2, C3FP, [p1, k1] 3 times, p1, C3BP, p6.

12th row As 8th row.

13th row P7, C3FP, [p1, k1] twice, p1, C3BP, p4, C3FP, [p1, k1] twice, p1, C3BP, p7.

14th row As 6th row.

15th row P8, C3FP, p1, k1, p1, C3BP, p6, C3FP, p1, k1, p1, C3BP, p8.

16th row As 4th row.

17th row P9, C3FP, p1, C3BP, p8, C3FP, p1, C3BP, p9.

18th row As 2nd row.

19th to 38th rows Rep 1st to 18th rows once more then 1st and 2nd rows again.

motif D
(worked over 40 sts)

1st row P8, k2, p8, C4B, p8, k2, p8.

2nd row K8, p2, k8, p4, k8, p2, k8.

3rd row P8, C4FP, p4, C4BP, C4FP, p4, C4BP, p8.

4th row K10, [p2, k4] 3 times, p2, k10.

5th row P10, C4FP, C4BP, p4, C4FP, C4BP, p10.

6th row K12, p4, k8, p4, k12.

7th row P12, C4B, p4, MB, p3, C4F, p12.

8th row As 6th row.

9th row P10, C4BP, C4FP, p4, C4BP, C4FP, p10.

10th row As 4th row.

11th row P8, C4BP, p4, C4FP, C4BP, p4, C4FP, p8.

12th row As 2nd row.

13th row P8, k2, p4, MB, p3, C4B, p4, MB, p3, k2, p8.

14th row K8, p2, k8, p4, k8, p2, k8.

15th to 26th rows Rep 3rd to 14th rows once more.

27th to 36th rows Rep 3rd to 12th rows.

37th and 38th rows As 1st and 2nd rows.

to make

With 3mm circular needle and M, cast on 240 sts.
K 19 rows.
1st row K10, [p1, k1] to last 12 sts, p1, k11.
2nd row K11, [p1, k1] to last 11 sts, p1, k10.
Rep the last 2 rows 3 times more.
Change to 3.25mm circular needle.

First row of motifs
1st row (right side) K10, moss st 5, [p38, moss st 5] to last 53 sts, k38, moss st 5, k10.
2nd row K10, moss st 5, p38, moss st 5, [k38, moss st 5] to last 10 sts, k10.
3rd row As 1st row.
4th (inc) row (wrong side) K10, moss st 5, p38, moss st 5, k18, m1, k2, m1, k18, moss st 5, k11, m1, k16, m1, k11, moss st, 5, k18, m1, k2, m1, k18, moss st 5, k10, m1, k18, m1, k10, moss st 5, k10. 248 sts.
5th row K10, moss st 5, work across 1st row of motif A, moss st 5, work across 1st row of motif D, moss st 5, work across 1st row of motif C, moss st 5, work across 1st row of motif B, moss st 5, k38, moss st 5, k10.
6th row K10, moss st 5, p38, moss st 5, work across 2nd row of motif B, moss st 5, work across 2nd row of motif C, moss st 5, work across 2nd row of motif D, moss st 5, work across 2nd row of motif A, moss st 5, k10.
The last 2 rows set the position of the motifs with moss st between and garter st edging.
Working correct patt rows, work a further 36 rows.
43rd (dec) row K10, moss st 5, p9, p2tog, p18, p2tog, p9, moss st 5, p18, [p2tog] twice, p18, moss st 5, p10, p2tog, p16, p2tog, p10, moss st 5, p18, [p2tog] twice, p18, moss st 5, k38, moss st 5, k10. 240 sts.
44th row K10, moss st 5, p38, moss st 5, [k38, moss st 5] to last 10 sts, k10.
45th and 46th rows As 1st and 2nd rows.
Change to 3mm circular needle.
1st row K10, [p1, k1] to last 12 sts, p1, k11.
2nd row K11, [p1, k1] to last 11 sts, p1, k10.
Rep the last 2 rows 3 times more.
Change to 3.25mm circular needle.

** Second row of motifs
1st row (right side) K10, moss st 5, [p38, moss st 5] to last 10 sts, k10.
2nd row K10, moss st 5, [k38, moss st 5] to last 10 sts, k10.
3rd row As 1st row.
4th (inc) row (wrong side) K10, moss st 5, k18, m1, k2, m1, k18, moss st 5, k11, m1, k16, m1, k11, moss st 5, k18, m1, k2, m1, k18, moss st 5, k10, m1, k18, m1, k10, moss st 5, k18, m1, k2, m1, k18, moss st 5, k10. 250 sts.
5th row K10, moss st 5, work across 1st row of motif B, moss st 5, work across 1st row of motif A, moss st 5, work across 1st row of motif D, moss st 5, work across 1st row of motif C, moss st 5, work across 1st row of motif B, moss st 5, k10.
6th row K10, moss st 5, work across 2nd row of motif B, moss st 5, work across 2nd row of motif C, moss st 5, work across 2nd row of motif D, moss st 5, work across 2nd row of motif A, moss st 5, work across 2nd row of motif B, moss st 5, k10.
The last 2 rows set the position of the motifs with moss st between and garter st edging.

Working correct patt rows, work a further 36 rows.

43rd (dec) row K10, moss st 5, p18, [p2tog] twice, p18, moss st 5, p9, p2tog, p18, p2tog, p9, moss st 5, p18, [p2tog] twice, p18, moss st 5, p10, p2tog, p16, p2tog, p10, moss st 5, p18, [p2tog] twice, p18, moss st 5, k10. 240 sts.

44th row K10, moss st 5, [k38, moss st 5] to last 10 sts, k10.

45th and 46th rows As 1st and 2nd rows.

Change to 3mm circular needle.

1st row K10, [p1, k1] to last 12 sts, p1, k11.

2nd row K11, [p1, k1] to last 11 sts, p1, k10.

Rep the last 2 rows 3 times more.

Change to 3.25mm circular needle.

Third row of motifs

1st row (right side) K10, moss st 5, [p38, moss st 5] to last 10 sts, k10.

2nd row K10, moss st 5, [k38, moss st 5] to last 10 sts, k10.

3rd row As 1st row.

4th (inc) row (wrong side) K10, moss st 5, k11, m1, k16, m1, k11, moss st, 5, k18, m1, k2, m1, k18, moss st 5, k10, m1, k18, m1, k10, moss st 5, k18, m1, k2, m1, k18, moss st 5, k11, m1, k16, m1, k11, moss st 5, k10. 250 sts.

5th row K10, moss st 5, work across 1st row of motif C, moss st 5, work across 1st row of motif B, moss st 5, work across 1st row of motif A, moss st 5, work across 1st row of motif D, moss st 5, work across 1st row of motif C, moss st 5, k10.

6th row K10, moss st 5, work across 2nd row of motif C, moss st 5, work across 2nd row of motif D, moss st 5, work across 2nd row of motif A, moss st 5, work across 2nd row of motif B, moss st 5, work across 2nd row of motif C, moss st 5, k10.

These 2 rows set the position of the motifs with moss st between and garter st edging.

Working correct patt rows, work a further 36 rows.

43rd (dec) row K10, moss st 5, p10, p2tog, p16, p2tog, p10, moss st 5, p18, [p2tog] twice, p18, moss st 5, p9, p2tog, p18, p2tog, p9, moss st 5, p18, [p2tog] twice, p18, moss st 5, p10, p2tog, p16, p2tog, p10, moss st 5, k10. 240 sts.

44th row K10, moss st 5, [k38, moss st 5] to last 10 sts, k10.

45th and 46th rows As 1st and 2nd rows.

Change to 3mm circular needle.

1st row K10, [p1, k1] to last 12 sts, p1, k11.

2nd row K11, [p1, k1] to last 11 sts, p1, k10.

Rep the last 2 rows 3 times more. **

Change to 3.25mm circular needle.

Fourth row of motifs

1st row (right side) K10, moss st 5, [p38, moss st 5] to last 10 sts, k10.

2nd row K10, moss st 5, [k38, moss st 5] to last 10 sts, k10.

3rd row As 1st row.

4th (inc) row (wrong side) K10, moss st, 5, k18, m1, k2, m1, k18, moss st 5, k10, m1, k18, m1, k10, moss st 5, k18, m1, k2, m1, k18, moss st 5, k11, m1, k16, m1, k11, moss st 5, k18, m1, k2, m1, k18, moss st 5, k10. 250 sts

5th row K10, work across 1st row of motif D, moss st 5, work across 1st row of motif C, moss st 5,

work across 1st row of motif B, moss st 5, work across 1st row of motif A, moss st 5, work across 1st row of motif D, moss st 5, k10.

6th row K10, moss st 5, work across 2nd row of motif D, moss st 5, work across 2nd row of motif A, moss st 5, work across 2nd row of motif B, moss st 5, work across 2nd row of motif C, moss st 5, work across 2nd row of motif D, moss st 5, k10.

The last 2 rows set the position of the motifs with moss st between and garter st edging.

Working correct patt rows, work a further 36 rows.

43rd (dec) row K10, moss st 5, p18, [p2tog] twice, p18, moss st 5, p10, p2tog, p16, p2tog, p10, moss st 5, p18, [p2tog] twice, p18, moss st 5, p9, p2tog, p18, p2tog, p9, moss st 5, p18, [p2tog] twice, p18, moss st 5, k10. 240 sts.

44th row K10, moss st 5, [k38, moss st 5] to last 10 sts, k10.

45th and 46th rows As 1st and 2nd rows.

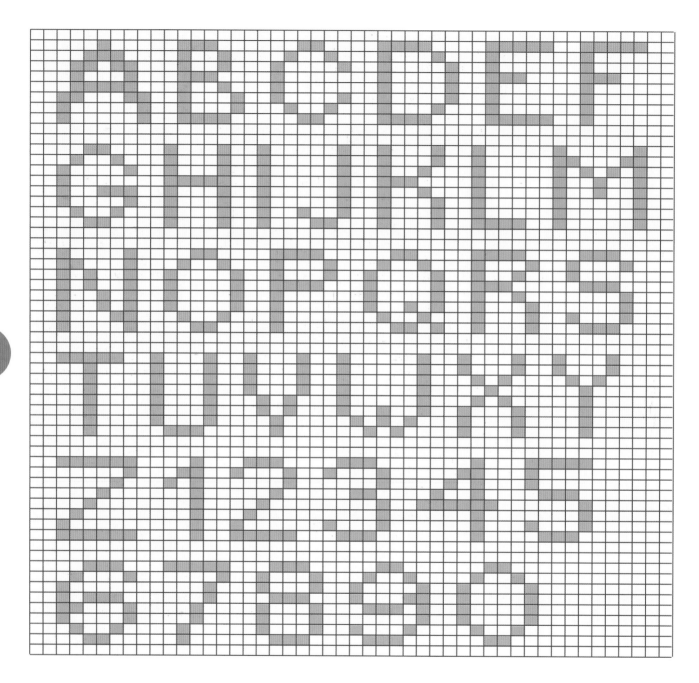

Change to 3mm circular needle.

1st row K10, [p1, k1] to last 12 sts, p1, k11.

2nd row K11, [p1, k1] to last 11 sts, p1, k10.

Rep the last 2 rows 3 times more.

Change to 3.25mm circular needle.

Fifth row of motifs

1st row (right side) K10, moss st 5, [p38, moss st 5] to last 10 sts, k10.

2nd row K10, moss st 5, [k38, moss st 5] to last 10 sts, k10.

3rd row As 1st row.

4th (inc) row (wrong side) K10, moss st 5, k10, m1, k18, m1, k10, moss st 5, k18, m1, k2, m1, k18, moss st 5, k11, m1, k16, m1, k11, moss st 5, k18, m1, k2, m1, k18, moss st 5, k10, m1, k18, m1, k10, moss st 5, k10. 250 sts.

5th row K10, moss st 5, work across 1st row of motif A, moss st 5, work across 1st row of motif D, moss st 5, work across 1st row of motif C, moss st 5, work across 1st row of motif B, moss st 5, work across 1st row of motif A, moss st 5, k10.

6th row K10, moss st 5, work across 2nd row of motif A, moss st 5, work across 2nd row of motif B, moss st 5, work across 2nd row of motif C, moss st 5, work across 2nd row of motif D, moss st 5, work across 2nd row of motif A, moss st 5, k10.

The last 2 rows set the position of the motifs with moss st between and garter st edging.

Working correct patt rows, work a further 36 rows.

43rd (dec) row K10, moss st 5, p9, p2tog, p18, p2tog, p9, moss st 5, p18, [p2tog] twice, p18, moss st 5, p10, p2tog, p16, p2tog, p10, moss st 5, p18, [p2tog] twice, p18, moss st 5, p9, p2tog, p18, p2tog, p9, moss st 5, k10. 240 sts.

44th row K10, moss st 5, [k38, moss st 5] to last 10 sts, k10.

45th and 46th rows As 1st and 2nd rows.

Change to 3mm circular needle.

1st row K10, [p1, k1] to last 12 sts, p1, k11.

2nd row K11, [p1, k1] to last 11 sts, p1, k10.

Rep the last 2 rows 3 times more.

Change to 3.25mm circular needle.

Sixth and seventh rows of motifs

Work as Second and Third row of motifs from ** to **.

K 19 rows.

Cast off.

embroidery

Using your own selection of letters and numbers from the Chart opposite and contrast yarn (C), Swiss darn the initials and date onto the blank square at the lower left-hand corner.

size
Approximately 9cm high

materials
1 x 50g ball Debbie Bliss Baby Cashmerino in grey (A)
Oddments of Debbie Bliss Cashmerino Aran in each of charcoal (B) and gold (C)
Pair each 2.75mm and 4mm knitting needles

tension
29 sts and 42 rows to 10cm square over st st using 2.75mm needles.

abbreviations
sk2togpo = slip 1, k2tog, pass slipped st over.
Also see page 25.

body

With 2.75mm needles and A, cast on 26 sts.
Beg with a k row, work in st st until piece measures 18cm, ending with a k row.
Cast off.

beak

With 4mm needles and C, cast on 6 sts.
Next 2 rows K4, turn, sl 1, k3.
Next 2 rows K5, turn, sl 1, k4.
Next 2 rows K to end.
Next 2 rows K5, turn, sl 1, k4.
Next 2 rows K4, turn, sl 1, k3.
Cast off knitwise.
Join cast-on and cast-off edges.

feet (make 2)

With 4mm needles and B, cast on 13 sts.
1st and all wrong side rows K.
2nd row K5, sk2togpo, k5.
4th row K4, sk2togpo, k4.
6th row K3, sk2togpo, k3.
Cast off rem 7 sts.

to make up

Join cast-on and cast-off edges of body to form a tube. Fold the tube flat with the seam to one side and join from the seam to the fold. On the open edge, place a marker on the fold. Re-fold and match the cast-on/cast-off seam to the fold marker and join the open edges, leaving a gap large enough to insert stuffing. Stuff and close gap in seam. Position beak on bird and sew in place firmly. Position feet on bird and sew in place securely. With B, sew a few sts to form eyes.

little bird toy

big bird cushion

size
Approximately 85cm high

materials
19 x 50g balls of Debbie Bliss Rialto Aran in charcoal (A)
1 x 50g ball of Debbie Bliss Cashmerino Aran in each of mid grey (B) and yellow (C)
5mm circular knitting needle
Pair each 4mm and 4.5mm needles
93 x 156cm fabric for lining
Polystyrene beads
Wadding for beak and feet
Scraps of black felt for eyes

tension
18 sts and 24 rows to 10cm square over st st using 5mm needles.

abbreviations
sk2togpo = slip 1, k2tog, pass slipped st over.
Also see page 25.

note
The knitted piece is slightly smaller than the inner lining to prevent sagging.

to make

With 5mm circular needle and A, cast on 156 sts.
Beg with a k row, work in st st until piece measures 150cm.
Cast off.

beak

With 4mm needles and C, cast on 27 sts.
K 15 rows.
Next row (right side) K6, sk2togpo, k6. K 5 rows.
Next row K5, sk2togpo, k5. K 5 rows.
Next row K4, sk2togpo, k4. K 6 rows.
Cast off knitwise.

feet (make 4)

With 4.5mm needles and B, cast on 61 sts.
1st and all wrong side rows K.
2nd row K29, sk2togpo, k29.
4th row K28, sk2togpo, k28.
6th row K27, sk2togpo, k27.
Cont in this way, decreasing 2 sts on every right side row until 23 sts rem, ending with a RS row.
Cast off knitwise.

to make lining

Cut a piece of fabric 93 x 156cm. With right sides together and taking 1.5cm seams throughout, join the short sides of fabric piece together to form a tube (this seam forms the base of the bird). Fold the tube flat with the seam to one side and join from the seam to the fold (this forms the back of the bird). Open out the unstitched side and refold the fabric so the first sea lies centrally, and stitch the seam, leaving 5cm unstitched at one end. Turn through to the right side and fill with polystyrene beads. Stitch the opening closed.

to make up

Join cast-on and cast-off edges of knitted piece to form a tube (this seam forms the base of the bird). Fold the tube flat with the seam to one side and join from the seam to the fold (this seam forms the back of the bird). On the open edge, place a marker on the fold. Open out the unstitched side and insert the filled lining; then matching the first seam (base) to the marker, stitch the seam closed so that the first seam lies centrally. Join row ends of beak, then fold beak in half with seam to centre of cast-off edge and then join to form end of beak. Cut pieces of wadding and place inside beak, then securely sew to the front of the bird. Using one of the feet as a template, cut pieces of wadding slightly smaller than knitted foot. Join the feet in pairs with the wadding in the centre. Position the feet on the bird and stitch in place. Cut two 2cm circles of felt for eyes and stitch in place.

fairisle
hangers

size
To fit a 22cm plain wooden coathanger

materials
1 x 50g ball (or oddments) Debbie Bliss Baby Cashmerino in each of pale pink, lime, teal, duck egg, ecru, red and pink
Pair 3.25mm knitting needles
22cm plain wooden coathangers
Polyester wadding
30cm of narrow ribbon

tension
25 sts and 34 rows to 10cm over fairisle st st using 3.25mm needles.

abbreviations
See page 25.

note
You may find it difficult to obtain 22cm coathangers, but you can easily down a standard width hanger to size using a hacksaw. If you want to cover a hanger of a different width, you will need to recalculate the number of sts. The pattern is worked over a multiple of 8 sts, plus 1 edge st.

to make

With 3.25mm needles and main colour from your chosen chart, cast on 57 sts.
Beg with a k row, work 2 rows in st st.
Now cont in st st and work from chart as follows:
1st chart row (right side) K1 edge st, [k8 patt rep sts] 7 times.
2nd chart row [P8 patt rep sts] 7 times, p1 edge st.
These 2 rows set the position of the chart and are repeated.
Cont until all 15 chart rows have been worked, then rep these 15 rows once more.
Cast off.

to finish

Pad a coathanger with wadding and stitch in place. Fold knitting in half matching cast-on and cast-off edges and join side seams from fold to edge. Find the centre of the cover and thread hanger hook through at this point. Ease cover over hanger and join cast-on to cast-off edges. Tie a ribbon around base of hook.

| pale pink | lime | teal | duck egg | ecru | red | pink |

8 st repeat — edge st

8 st repeat — edge st

8 st repeat — edge st

size
Approximately 25 (42)cm high

materials
Little bear 2 x 50g balls Debbie Bliss Baby Cashmerino in stone (A)
Pair 2.75mm knitting needles
Big bear 4 x 50g balls Debbie Bliss Cashmerino Chunky in stone (B)
Pair 5mm knitting needles
Oddments of chocolate yarn for embroidery
1m of 1.5cm wide ribbon for each bear
Washable toy stuffing (see Note on page 47)
Scraps of chocolate felt and matching sewing thread

tension
28 sts and 58 rows in Baby Cashmerino (A) using 2.75mm needles and 18 sts and 38 rows in
Cashmerino Chunky (B) using 5mm needles, both to 10cm square over garter st.

big & little bear

abbreviations
See page 25.

notes
Both bears are worked in garter stitch (k every row).
Little bear is made using Baby Cashmerino and 2.75mm knitting needles throughout.
Big bear is made using Cashmerino Chunky and 5mm needles throughout.
All the instructions are for both bears, different needles and yarns create the size difference.

body

The body is worked starting at the neck edge.
With 2.75mm (5mm) needles and A (B), cast on 12 sts and k 1 row.

Shape shoulders

Next row Cast on 2 sts, k to end.

Rep this row 3 times more. 20 sts. K 4 rows.

Next row K1, m1, k to last st, m1, k1. 22 sts. K 5 rows. **

Rep the last 6 rows 5 times more. 32 sts.

Shape base

Next row K1, [ssk, k11, k2tog] twice, k1. 28 sts. K 1 row.

Next row K1, [ssk, k9, k2tog] twice, k1. 24 sts. K 1 row.

*** **Next row** K1, [ssk, k7, k2tog] twice, k1. 20 sts. K 1 row.

Cont to dec 4 sts in this way on every alt row until 8 sts rem.

Next row K1, sl 1, k2tog, psso, k3tog, k1. 4 sts.

Next row [K2tog] twice. 2 sts.

Next row K2tog and fasten off.

body front

Work as Body Back to **.
Next row K1, m1, k to last st, m1, k1. 24 sts. K 5 rows.
Next row K1, m1, k10, m1, k2, m1, k10, m1, k1. 28 sts. K 5 rows.
Next row K1, m1, k10, m1, k6, m1, k10, m1, k1. 32 sts. K 5 rows.
Next row K1, m1, k to last st, m1, k1. 34 sts. K 5 rows.
Rep the last 6 rows once more. 36 sts.
Next row K1, ssk, k6, ssk, k5, k2tog, ssk, k5, k2tog, k6, k2tog, k1. 30 sts. K 1 row.
Next row K1, ssk, k5, ssk, k3, k2tog, ssk, k3, k2tog, k5, k2tog, k1. 24 sts. K 1 row.
Now work as Body Back from *** to end.

head

With 2.75mm (5mm) needles and A (B), cast on 4 sts.
1st row K.
2nd row K1, [m1, k1] to end. 7 sts.
Rep the last 2 rows once more. 13 sts.
5th, 7th, 9th and 11th rows K.
6th row [K1, m1, k5, m1] twice, k1. 17 sts.
8th row K1, m1, k6, m1, k3, m1, k6, m1, k1. 21 sts.
10th row K1, m1, k7, m1, k5, m1, k7, m1, k1. 25 sts.
12th row K1, m1, k8, m1, k7, m1, k8, m1, k1. 29 sts. K 2 rows.
15th row K2, [ssk, k1] 3 times, k8, [k2tog, k1] 3 times, k1. 23 sts.
16th row K4, m1, k3, m1, k9, m1, k3, m1, k4. 27 sts. K 3 rows.
20th row [K4, m1] twice, k11, [m1, k4] twice. 31 sts. K 3 rows.
24th row K4, m1, k5, m1, k13, m1, k5, m1, k4. 35 sts. K 1 row.
26th row K4, m1, k6, m1, k15, m1, k6, m1, k4. 39 sts. K 1 row.
28th row K4, m1, k7, m1, k17, m1, k7, m1, k4. 43 sts. K 1 row.
30th row K3, [m1, k4] 3 times, m1, k13, m1, [k4, m1] 3 times, k3. 51 sts. K 12 rows.
43rd row K9, k2tog, [k8, k2tog] 4 times. 46 sts. K 1 row.
45th row K8, k2tog, [k7, k2tog] 4 times. 41 sts. K 1 row.
47th row K7, k2tog, [k6, k2tog] 4 times. 36 sts. K 1 row.
Dec 5 sts in this way on next row and 4 foll alt rows. 11 sts. K 1 row.
Next row Sl 1, k2tog, psso, [k2tog] 4 times. 5 sts.
Break yarn, thread through rem sts, pull up and secure.
Join seam, leaving a gap. Stuff carefully and close gap in seam.

ears (make 2)

With 2.75mm (5mm) needles and A (B), cast on 11 sts. K 3 rows.
4th row K1, ssk, k5, k2tog, k1. K 1 row.
6th row K1, ssk, k3, k2tog, k1. K 1 row.
8th row K1, ssk, k1, k2tog, k1. 5 sts. K 1 row.
10th row K1, m1, k3, m1, k1. K 1 row.
12th row K1, m1, k5, m1, k1. K 1 row.
14th row K1, m1, k7, m1, k1. 11 sts. K 2 rows.
Cast off.
Fold in half and slip stitch around edge.

legs (make 2)

big bear sole
cut 2

With 2.75mm (5mm) needles and A (B), cast on 15 sts. K 1 row.
2nd row K1, m1, k4, m1, k1, m1, k3, m1, k1, m1, k4, m1, k1. 21 sts. K 1 row.
4th row K1, m1, k6, m1, k2, m1, k3, m1, k2, m1, k6, m1, k1. 27 sts. K 1 row.
6th row K9, m1, k3, [m1, k1] 3 times, m1, k3, m1, k9. 33 sts. K 9 rows.
16th row K12, ssk, k5, k2tog, k12. 31 sts. K 1 row.
18th row K12, ssk, k3, k2tog, k12. 29 sts. K 1 row.
20th row K12, ssk, k1, k2tog, k12. 27 sts. K 1 row.
22nd row K11, ssk, k1, k2tog, k11. 25 sts. K 1 row.
24th row K10, ssk, k1, k2tog, k10. 23 sts. K 1 row.
26th row K9, ssk, k1, k2tog, k9. 21 sts. K 28 rows.
56th row K4, ssk, k9, k2tog, k4. 19 sts. K 1 row.
58th row K4, ssk, k7, k2tog, k4. 17 sts. K 1 row.
60th row K2, ssk, k2tog, k5, ssk, k2tog, k2. 13 sts. K 1 row.
62nd row K1, ssk, k2tog, sl 2tog, k1, pass 2 slipped sts over, ssk, k2tog, k1. 7 sts. K 1 row.
64th row K1, ssk, k1, k2tog, k1. 5 sts.
Break yarn, thread through rem sts, pull up and secure.

arms (make 2)

big bear paw
cut 2

With 2.75mm (5mm) needles and A (B), cast on 7 sts. K 1 row.
2nd row [K1, m1, k2, m1] twice, k1. 11 sts. K 1 row.
4th row K1, m1, [k3, m1] 3 times, k1. 15 sts. K 1 row.
6th row K1, m1, k4, m1, k5, m1, k4, m1, k1. 19 sts. K 1 row.
8th row K1, m1, k17, m1, k1. 21 sts. K 1 row.
10th row K1, m1, k7, ssk, k1, k2tog, k7, m1, k1. 21 sts. K 1 row.
Rep the last 2 rows once more.
14th row K8, ssk, k1, k2tog, k8. 19 sts. K 1 row.
16th row K7, ssk, k1, k2tog, k7. 17 sts. K 24 rows.
41st row K2, ssk, k2tog, k5, ssk, k2tog, k2. 13 sts. K 1 row.
43rd row K1, ssk, k2tog, sl 2tog, k1, pass 2 slipped sts over, ssk, k2tog, k1. 7 sts. K 1 row.
45th row K1, ssk, k1, k2tog, k1. 5 sts.
Break yarn, thread through rem sts, pull up and secure.

to make up

Join body back to body front leaving neck edge open. Stuff firmly and run a thread around neck edge, pull up slightly and fasten off. Sew ears to head. Embroider facial features with chocolate yarn. Sew head to body at neck. Fold each arm and each leg in half, join seam, leaving a gap, stuff firmly and close gap. Sew arms and legs in place to body. Tie ribbon around neck in a bow and trim ends. Using the templates, cut paw and foot pads from felt and sew in place.

little bear
sole
cut 2

little
bear paw
cut 2

122 memory book cover

size
To fit a 21 x 16cm notebook

materials
2 x 50g balls Debbie Bliss Baby Cashmerino in silver (A), 1 x 50g ball in ecru (B) and oddments
in pale pink (C)
Pair 3.25mm knitting needles
Oddment of chocolate six-strand embroidery thread
4 small mother-of-pearl buttons (optional)
21 x 16cm notebook

tension
25 sts and 34 rows to 10cm square over st st using 3.25mm needles.

abbreviations
See page 25.

note
The memory book cover is worked sideways starting at the inside back cover.

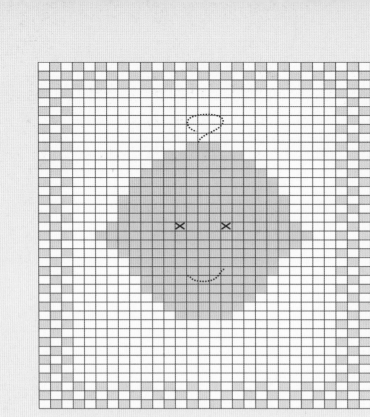

With B, k on right side rows, p on wrong side rows

With B, p on right side rows, k on wrong side rows

With C, k on right side rows, p on wrong side rows

Embroider on completion

pattern A

1st row (right side) [K1, p1] twice, k to last 4 sts, [p1, k1] twice.
2nd row K1, [p1, k1] twice, p to last 5 sts, [k1, p1] twice, k1.
These 2 rows form st st with moss st edges and are repeated.

cover

With 3.25mm needles and A, cast on 55 sts.
Moss st row (right side) K1, [p1, k1] to end.
Rep this row 3 times more.
Work 21 rows in patt A, so ending with a 1st row.
Foldline row (wrong side) K1, p1, k to last 2 sts, p1, k1.
Work 6 rows in moss st.
Work 45 rows in patt A, so ending with a 1st row.
Work 21 rows in moss st.
Work 45 rows in patt A, so ending with a 1st row.
Work 6 rows in moss st.
Foldline row (wrong side) K1, p1, k to last 2 sts, p1, k1.
Work 21 rows in patt A, so ending with a 1st row.
Next row K1, [p1, k1] to end.
Work 4 rows in moss st.
Cast off in moss st.

front patch

With 3.25mm needles and B, cast on 29 sts.
Beg with a right side row, work 39 rows in patt from Chart.
Cast off in moss st.
Embroider features using 3 strands of stranded embroidery thread.

to make up

Stitch patch to front cover and decorate with a small button in each corner. Fold cover along foldline rows and stitch inside cover flaps to outside cover along edges.

striped cardigan

measurements
To fit ages 3–6 (6–9: 9–12: 12–18: 18–24) months
actual measurements
Chest 51 (56: 60: 65: 70)cm
Length to shoulder 24 (26: 28: 32: 36)cm
Sleeve length 15 (17: 19: 22: 24)cm

materials
2 (2: 2: 3: 3) x 50g balls Debbie Bliss Baby Cashmerino in each of grey (M) and ecru (C)
Pair each 3mm and 3.25mm knitting needles
3mm circular knitting needle
6 (6: 6: 7: 7) buttons

tension
25 sts and 34 rows to 10cm square over st st using 3.25mm needles.

abbreviations
See page 25.

back

With 3mm needles and C, cast on 65 (71: 77: 83: 89) sts.
1st rib row K1, [p1, k1] to end.
Change to M.
2nd rib row P1, [k1, p1] to end.
With M, rep the last 2 rows twice more.
Change to 3.25mm needles.
Beg with a k row, work in st st and stripes of 2 rows C and 2 rows M, until back measures
14 (15: 16: 19: 22)cm from cast-on edge, ending with a p row.
Shape armholes
Keeping st st stripes correct as set throughout, cast off 3 (3: 3: 4: 4) sts at beg of next 2 rows.
Next row K2, skpo, k to last 4 sts, k2tog, k2.
Next row P to end.
Rep the last 2 rows 3 (4: 5: 5: 6) times. 51 (55: 59: 63: 67) sts.
Cont straight until back measures 24 (26: 28: 32: 36)cm from cast-on edge, ending with a p row.
Shape shoulders
Cast off 12 (13: 14: 15: 16) sts at beg of next 2 rows.
Leave rem 27 (29: 31: 33: 35) sts on a holder.

left front

With 3mm needles and C, cast on 33 (35: 39: 41: 45) sts.
1st rib row P1, [k1, p1] to end.
Change to M.
2nd rib row K1, [p1, k1] to end.
With M, rep the last 2 rows twice more.
Change to 3.25mm needles. **
Beg with a k row, work in st st and stripes of 2 rows C and 2 rows M until front measures
14 (15: 16: 19: 22)cm from cast-on edge, ending with the same stripe row as Back.
Shape armhole
Keeping st st stripes correct as set throughout, cast off 3 (3: 3: 4: 4) sts at beg of next row.
Work 1 row.
Next row K2, skpo, k to end.
Next row P to end.
Rep the last 2 rows 3 (4: 5: 5: 6) times. 26 (27: 30: 31: 34) sts.
Cont straight until front measures 19 (21: 22: 26: 29)cm from cast-on edge, ending with a p row.
Shape neck
Next row K to last 4 (5: 5: 5: 6) sts and leave these sts on a holder.
Dec 1 st at neck edge on every row until 12 (13: 14: 15: 16) sts rem.
Cont straight until front measures same as Back to shoulder, ending at armhole edge.
Shape shoulder
Cast off.

right front

Work as given for Left Front to **.
Beg with a k row, cont in st st and stripes of 2 rows C and 2 rows M until front measures
14 (15: 16: 19: 22)cm from cast-on edge, working one more row than on Left Front.
Shape armhole
Keeping st st stripes correct as set throughout, cast off 3 (3: 3: 4: 4) sts at beg of next row.
Next row K to last 4 sts, k2tog, k2.
Next row P to end.
Rep the last 2 rows 3 (4: 5: 5: 6) times. 26 (27: 30: 31: 34) sts.
Cont straight until front measures 19 (21: 22: 26: 29)cm from cast-on edge, ending with a p row.
Shape neck
Next row K4 (5: 5: 5: 6) sts, leave these sts on a holder, k to end.
Dec 1 st at neck edge on every row until 12 (13: 14: 15: 16) sts rem.
Cont straight until front measures same as Back to shoulder, ending at armhole edge.
Shape shoulder
Cast off.

sleeves

With 3mm needles and C, cast on 34 (36: 38: 40: 42) sts.
1st rib row [K1, p1] to end.
Change to M.
With M, rep the last row 5 times more.
Change to 3.25mm needles.
Beg with a k row, work in st st and stripes of 2 rows C and 2 rows M and **at the same time** inc
1 st at each end of the 3rd row and every foll 4th row until there are 54 (56: 60: 68: 74) sts.
Working in st st stripes as set throughout, cont straight until sleeve measures 15 (17: 19: 22:
24)cm from cast-on edge, ending with the same stripe row as on Back to armhole.
Shape sleeve top
Cast off 3 (3: 3: 4: 4) sts at beg of next 2 rows.
Next row K2, skpo, k to last 4 sts, k2tog, k2.
Next row P to end.
Rep the last 2 rows 3 (4: 5: 5: 6) times. 40 (40: 42: 48: 52) sts.
Cast off.

neckband

Join shoulder seams.
With right side facing, 3mm needles and M, slip 4 (5: 5: 5: 6) sts on right front holder onto a
needle, pick up and k17 (17: 18: 19: 19) sts up right front neck, k27 (29: 31: 33: 35) sts from back
neck holder, pick up and k17 (17: 18: 19: 19) sts down left front neck, then k4 (5: 5: 5: 6) sts from
left front holder. 69 (73: 77: 81: 85) sts.
1st row P1, [k1, p1] to end.
2nd row K1, [p1, k1] to end.
These 2 rows form the rib.
Work 3 rows more in rib.
Change to C.
Rib 1 row.
Cast off in rib.

button band	With right side facing, 3mm needles and M, pick up and k55 (61: 63: 71: 77) sts along left front edge. Work 5 rows in rib as given for Neckband. Change to C. Rib 1 row. Cast off in rib.
buttonhole band	With right side facing, 3mm needles and M, pick up and k55 (61: 63: 71: 77) sts along right front edge. Work 2 rows in rib as given for Neckband. **Buttonhole row** Rib 1 (2: 3: 1: 1), [rib 2tog, yf, rib 8 (9: 9: 9: 10) sts] 5 (5: 5: 6: 6) times, rib 2tog, yf, rib 2 (2: 3: 2: 2). Rib 2 rows. Change to C. Rib 1 row. Cast off in rib.
to make up	Sew sleeves into armholes, matching stripes on shaping and easing cast-off edge to fit. Join side and sleeve seams. Sew on buttons.

size
To fit ages 3–6 months

materials
1 x 50g ball Debbie Bliss Baby Cashmerino in each of grey (M) and ecru (C)
Pair 2.75mm knitting needles

tension
28 sts and 37 rows to 10cm square over st st using 2.75mm needles.

abbreviations
See page 25.

striped bootees

to make

With 2.75mm needles and M, cast on 36 sts and k 1 row.
1st row (right side) K1, yf, k16, yf, [k1, yf] twice, k16, yf, k1.
2nd and all wrong side rows K to end, working k1 tbl into each yf of previous row.
3rd row K2, yf, k16, yf, k2, yf, k3, yf, k16, yf, k2.
5th row K3, yf, k16, yf, [k4, yf] twice, k16, yf, k3.
7th row K4, yf, k16, yf, k5, yf, k6, yf, k16, yf, k4.
9th row K5, yf, k16, yf, [k7, yf] twice, k16, yf, k5.
11th row K22, yf, k8, yf, k9, yf, k22. 64 sts.
12th row As 2nd row.
Beg with a k row, cont in st st stripes of 2 rows C, 2 rows M throughout as follows:
Work 10 rows.
Shape instep
Next row K36, skpo, turn.
Next row Sl 1, p8, p2tog, turn.
Next row Sl 1, k8, skpo, turn.
Rep the last 2 rows 7 times more, then work first of the 2 rows again.
Next row Sl 1, k to end.
Next row P17, p2tog, p8, p2tog tbl, p17. 44 sts.
Break off C and cont in M only.
Next row [K1, p1] to end.
Rep the last row 11 times more.
Change to C.
Rib 1 row and cast off in rib.

to finish

Join sole and back seam.

buildingblocks

size
Each block measures approximately 7.5 x 7.5 x 7.5cm

materials
1 x 50g ball Debbie Bliss Baby Cashmerino in each of indigo (A), duck egg (B), lime (C), raspberry (D), silver (E) and camel (F)
Oddments of brown yarn for embroidery
Pair 3mm knitting needles
5 foam blocks, each 7.5 x 7.5 x 7.5cm

tension
26 sts and 36 rows over st st to 10cm square using 3mm needles.

abbreviations
See page 25.

note
Each of the five blocks of the building blocks set is made from six different knitted faces.

plain face
(make 5)

With 3mm needles and A, cast on 19 sts.
Moss st row K1, [p1, k1] to end.
Rep the moss st row 31 times more.
Cast off in moss st.
Make 4 more plain faces in same way, working one in each of B, C, D and E.

narrow stripe face (make 5)

With 3mm needles and A, cast on 19 sts.
Work in garter st stripe sequence as follows:
* K 1 row A, 2 rows B, 2 rows C, 2 rows D, 2 rows E, 2 rows F, 1 row A; rep from * twice more,
then k 1 row A, 2 rows B, 2 rows C, 1 row D.
Cast off knitwise in D.
Make 4 more narrow stripe faces in same way.

wide stripe face (make 5)

With 3mm needles and A, cast on 19 sts.
Beg with a k row, work 27 rows in st st in stripe sequence as follows:
3 rows A, 1 row B, 1 row A, 3 rows B, 1 row C, 1 row B, 3 rows C, 1 row D, 1 row C, 3 rows D,
1 row E, 1 row D, 3 rows E, 1 row F, 1 row E, 2 rows F.
Cast off knitwise in F.
Make 4 more wide stripe faces in same way.

bear face
(make 5)

With 3mm needles and E, cast on 19 sts.
Beg with a k row, work 28 rows in st st from bear chart on page 140, using E for background
and F for bear.
Cast off purlwise.
Embroider eyes, snout and mouth with brown yarn.
Make 4 more bear faces in same way, using F for all the bears and A or E for background.

bird's-eye spot face (make 5)

With 3mm needles and background colour of your choice, cast on 19 sts.
Beg with a k row, work 28 rows in st st from bird's-eye spot chart using spot colour of your choice.
Cast off.
Make 4 more bird's-eye spot faces in same way, using a different colour combination for each one.

number face
(make 5)

With 3mm needles and background colour of your choice, cast on 19 sts.
Beg with a k row, work 28 rows in st st from number chart '1' using number colour of your choice.
Make 4 more number faces in same way, using a different number (2, 3, 4 and 5) and a different
colour combination for each one.

to make up

For each of the five blocks, select one of each of the six different faces and sew them together
as follows:
Join four faces together in a strip; then join the remaining two faces to the strip as shown in the
assembly diagram on page 140. Join the first face to the fourth face of the strip of four, then join
the remaining three sides of one of the side faces to the four. Insert the foam block and join the
remaining three sides to the four.

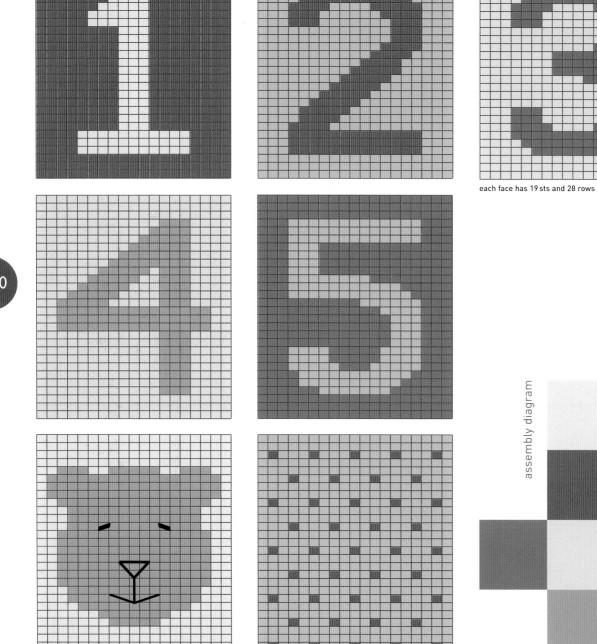

each face has 19 sts and 28 rows

assembly diagram

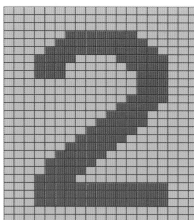

yarn distributors

For stockists of Debbie Bliss yarns please contact:

UK & WORLDWIDE DISTRIBUTORS
Designer Yarns Ltd
Units 8–10
Newbridge Industrial Estate
Pitt Street, Keighley
W. Yorkshire BD21 4PQ
UK
t: +44 (0) 1535 664222
f: +44 (0) 1535 664333
e: alex@designeryarns.uk.com
w: www.designeryarns.uk.com

USA
Knitting Fever Inc.
315 Bayview Avenue
Amityville
NY 11701
USA
t: +1 516 546 3600
f: +1 516 546 6871
w: www.knittingfever.com

CANADA
Diamond Yarns Ltd
155 Martin Ross Avenue Unit 3
Toronto
Ontario M3J 2L9
Canada
t: +1 416 736 6111
f: +1 416 736 6112
w: www.diamondyarn.com

MEXICO
Estambres Crochet SA de CV
Aaron Saenz 1891–7
Col. Santa Maria
Monterrey
N.L. 64650, Mexico
t: +52 (81) 8335 3870
e: abremer@redmundial.com.mx

BELGIUM/HOLLAND
Pavan
Thomas Van Theemsche
Meerlaanstraat 73
9860 Balegem (Oostrezele)
Belgium
t: +32 (0) 9 221 85 94
f: +32 (0) 9 221 56 62
e: pavan@pandora.be

DENMARK
Fancy Knit
Hovedvejen 71
8586 Oerum Djurs
Ramten, Denmark
t: +45 59 46 21 89
f: +45 59 46 8018
e: roenneburg@mail.dk

FINLAND
Priima Käsityötalo
Hämeentie 26
00530 Helsinki, Finland
t: +358 9 7318 0010
f: +358 9 7318 0009
e: info@priima.net
w: www.priima.fi

FRANCE
Laines Plassard
La Filature
71800 Varennes-sous-Dun
France
w: www.laines-plassard.com

GERMANY/AUSTRIA/
SWITZERLAND/LUXEMBOURG
Designer Yarns (Deutschland) GmbH
Sachsstraße 30
D-50259 Pulheim-Brauweiler
Germany
t: +49 (0) 2234 205453
f: +49 (0) 2234 205456
e: info@designeryarns.de
w: www.designeryarns.de

ICELAND
Storkurinn ehf
Laugavegi 59
101 Reykjavík, Iceland
t: +354 551 8258
f: +354 562 8252
e: storkurinn@simnet.is

SPAIN
Oyambre Needlework SL
Balmes, 200 At. 4
08006 Barcelona, Spain
t: +34 (0) 93 487 26 72
f: +34 (0) 93 218 66 94
e: info@oyambreonline.com

SWEDEN
Nysta garn och textil
Hogasvagen 20
S-131 47 Nacka, Sweden
t: +46 (0) 8 612 0330
e: info@nysta.se
w: www.nysta.se

RUSSIA
Taiga Publishing
ul. Srednaja Pervomajskaja 4/1
Moscow Russian Federation
105077
Russia
t: +7 (495) 786 8274
e: info@debbiebliss.ru

AUSTRALIA/NEW ZEALAND
Prestige Yarns Pty Ltd
PO Box 39
Bulli
NSW 2516, Australia
t: +61 (0) 2 4285 6669
e: info@prestigeyarns.com
w: www.prestigeyarns.com

TAIWAN
U-Knit
1F, 199-1 Sec
Zhong Xiao East Road
Taipei, Taiwan
t: +886 2 27527557
f: +886 2 27528556
e: shuindigo@hotmail.com

BRAZIL
Quatro Estacoes Com
Las Linhas e Acessorios Ltda
Av. Das Nacoes Unidas
12551-9 Andar
Cep 04578-000 Sao Paulo
Brazil
t: +55 11 3443 7736
e: cristina@4estacoeslas.com.br

For more information on my other books and yarns, please visit www.debbieblissonline.com

Editorial Director Jane O'Shea
Creative Director Mary Evans
Project Editor Lisa Pendreigh
Photographer Ulla Nyeman
Stylist Julie Mansfield
Illustrator Kate Simunek
Pattern Illustrator Bridget Bodoano
Production Director Vincent Smith
Production Controller Ruth Deary

First published in 2009 by
Quadrille Publishing Limited
Alhambra House
27–31 Charing Cross Road
London WC2H 0LS
www.quadrille.co.uk

Reprinted in 2009
10 9 8 7 6 5 4 3 2

Text and project designs © 2009 Debbie Bliss
Photography, design and layout © 2009
Quadrille Publishing Limited

British Library Cataloguing-in-Publication Data
A catalogue record for this book is available
from the British Library.

ISBN: 978 184400 736 3

Printed in China

144

acknowledgements

This book wouldn't have been possible without the generous collaboration of the following:

Rosy Tucker, who produced all the wonderful toys, big and little birds and the memory book.
Her practical and creative input is always invaluable. Also for the pattern checking.

Penny Hill, for her essential pattern compiling.

Jane O'Shea, **Lisa Pendreigh** and **Mary Evans** at Quadrille Publishing for being such a
wonderful team to work with.

Julie Mansfield for the perfect styling and overall look.

Ulla Nyeman for the beautiful photography.

Jo Gillingwater for the great job baby grooming.

And, of course, the fantastic babies: **Alara, Anwyn, Conor, Daisy, Dotty, Frankie, Jago, Laud,
Luca, Luna, Mimi, Monty, Reggie** and **Robyn**.

The knitters, for the huge effort they put into creating perfect knits under deadline
pressure: **Cynthia Brent, Barbara Clapham, Pat Church, Jacqui Dunt, Shirley Kennet,
Maisie Lawrence** and **Frances Wallace**.

My fantastic agent, **Heather Jeeves**.

The distributors, agents, retailers and knitters who support all my books and yarns with
such enthusiasm and make what I do possible.